Affirmed

Volume II

365 POSITIVE THOUGHTS AND ACTIONS TO START YOUR DAY

DR. CHERYL POLOTE-WILLIAMSON

AFFIRMED VOLUME II

Printed in the United States of America

ISBN: 978-1-953497-73-4 (Hardcover)
ISBN: 978-1-953497-76-5 (Paperback)

Library of Congress Control Number: 2023919143

Published by Cocoon to Wings Publishing
7810 Gall Blvd., #311
Zephyrhills, FL 33541
www.CocoontoWingsBooks.com
(813) 906-WING (9464)

Affirmed

Volume II

Acknowledgments

Heartfelt thanks to my loving husband of 31 years, Russell Williamson, Sr. Russ; you give me the space and confidence to fulfill all the dreams that God has placed inside of me without reservation or hesitation. Your love fuels me through the darkest days, and I am so grateful for you.

To our three beautiful children, Russ Jr., his wife, Hailey, Lauren, and Courtney, I thank you and love you. You have all been my safe place to land whenever the world was not so kind. You are all uniquely talented. Watching you grow from babies into adults has been my greatest joy. I am so grateful that God chose me to be your mother, and you have multiplied my joy by giving me Leah and Russ III, my precious grandbabies. Seeing their smiles is the greatest blessing.

To my loving parents, Benjamin and Gretta Polote, I say thank you. Mom and Daddy, you have shown me that anything is possible if I believe it and work to make it happen. You have taught me immeasurable valuable lessons. Because of those lessons, I am the woman I am today.

To my siblings and first best friends, Denise Polote-Kelly and Benjamin R. Polote, I thank you from the bottom of my heart. You two have supported all my dreams and let me know that it was okay to be myself unapologetically. Our bond has carried me through the ebbs and flows of life.

To my mentors, I want to thank each of you. I always tell my coaching clients that every coach needs a coach. I am incredibly blessed with so many. Cynt Marshall, Patricia Bailey, Niecy Nash Betts, Beverly Deitz, Joseph N. Bell, Curtis King, Dr. Wanda Bolton-Davis, and Alexandria

Barlowe. Thank you for being part of my village, I consider you family. Each of you has poured into me in countless ways. I am better, stronger, and wiser because I have each of you.

Lastly, but certainly not least, I must thank my Cheryl Magazine staff, Cheryl Polote-Williamson, LLC team, Williamson Media Group, my Butterfly Sisters, my media partners, Dr. Kerry Ann Zamore Byrd, my best friend Kimberly Bizor Tolbert, my stylist, Felicia Bell, Brand Manager, Alaina Pinkney and my make-up artist, Simon. You all play integral parts of my dream team. I am a movement by myself, but I am truly a force because of each of you. Thank you for believing in me and for making sure that I am ready for each speaking engagement, photo shoot, and event.

Monthly Themes

JANUARY: SELF-LOVE AND CARE

Focusing On Your Emotional Wellbeing and Mental Health

FEBRUARY: DIVINE TIMING AND GOD'S PLAN

Trusting God, The Process, and The Plan

MARCH: PHYSICAL HEALTH AND WELLBEING

Mastering Your Physical Wellness

APRIL: EMBRACING CHANGE AND CULTIVATING HEALTHY FRIENDSHIPS

Being Flexible and Adaptable Throughout the Seasons of Life

MAY: MARRIAGE, PARENTING AND FAMILY LIFE

Understanding God's Purpose for You and The People You Love

JUNE: CAREER AND FINANCES

Mastering The Art of Stewardship

JULY: SHARE YOUR GIFTS AND SHINE YOUR LIGHT

Walking Boldly in God's Purpose for Your Gifts and Talents

AUGUST: HEALING FROM PAST TRAUMA

Freeing Yourself from The Bondage of Your Past Pain

SEPTEMBER: IN HIS PRESENCE

Unlocking The Power of Cultivating Your Relationship with God

OCTOBER: UNAFRAID TO FAIL AND READY TO FLY

Shifting Your Mindset About Failure and The Reality of What It Means to Fail

NOVEMBER: GROWING IN GRATITUDE

Unlocking The Secret to True Joy and Fulfillment

DECEMBER: RENEWED FOCUS AND ENERGY FOR THE NEW YEAR

Walking In Your Authenticity and Divine Blessings as You Prepare for Another Year

From Cheryl's Heart

It's hard to believe that it's been seven years since the release of the first volume of *Affirmed*. Since its release, I have received an outpouring of messages of gratitude, love, and support from countless men and women who were inspired. The common theme from every message I received was that making daily affirmations a sacred part of their daily routine radically affected their lives and mindsets.

These affirmations are for and about YOU! It starts with YOU. I encourage you to likewise make these new words of affirmation a part of your daily routine. Find a quiet place where you can be alone and free from distraction and read one page per day aloud. Investing this time in yourself will radically change your mind and your outlook on life. **My vision is for you to utilize this book as a journey.** As you complete each day, write your thoughts and feelings on the pages. Go back and read the pages from previous days as well. As you progress, you will see the growth in your thoughts. Seeing your own transformation is truly magical and rewarding.

I have witnessed the power of positive affirmations in my life and in the lives of my family and friends. It brings me the deepest joy to be able to share this with you - my extended family. In this second edition, I provide themes for each month with the goal of helping you get more specific and intentional about your thoughts and the things you focus on. My prayer and hope for you is that you use the affirmations in this book to fuel the next chapter of your life, which will undoubtedly be the best one yet!

Let your Life be affirmed

January:

Self-Love and Care

Focusing On Your Emotional Wellbeing and Mental Health

A wise person once told me that beginning a new year is like walking into a dark room; you have no idea what to expect. We don't have a crystal ball to see the future, and even if we did—we wouldn't know what to do or how to handle certain situations until we are actually in them. The best thing we can do to combat the uncertainty of a new year is to ensure that our foundation is right. It all starts with you. You are the only thing and person that you can control, so it must start with you.

This month, focus on YOU and your relationship with yourself. Your relationship with yourself will directly mirror your relationships with others. When God made us, He said that we were good, and that is a great foundation to build and grow from. Any influence that has caused you to doubt yourself or not love yourself was not sent by God. Now is the time to dismantle limiting beliefs, negative thoughts, and self-doubt. As you take time to read each affirmation this month, start with the understanding that when God made you, He said you are good. Know that anything short of that is not true. It's time for renewed confidence and belief in yourself. It's time to focus on loving and caring for yourself. Watch the world around you change as you sharpen your greatest tool - you!

I embrace and accept all aspects of myself.

GENESIS 1:27 AND 31 (KJV)

"SO, GOD CREATED MAN IN HIS *OWN* IMAGE, IN THE IMAGE OF GOD CREATED HE HIM; MALE AND FEMALE CREATED HE THEM."

"AND GOD SAW EVERYTHING THAT HE HAD MADE, AND BEHOLD, *IT WAS* VERY GOOD. AND THE EVENING AND THE MORNING WERE THE SIXTH DAY."

Radical self-acceptance is one of the greatest gifts I can give myself. Once I have accepted myself just as I am, I can begin the process of becoming the best version of myself. When I can embrace myself, flaws and all, I can start to strengthen the areas that I require improvement. It becomes easier to embrace and accept every aspect of myself when I remember that I was created in God's image - and most importantly – that when He made me, He made no mistakes; He declared that I am good.

With unwavering faith, I surrender my worries to God, knowing that His wisdom will light my path.

HEBREWS 11:1 (ESV)

"NOW FAITH IS THE ASSURANCE OF THINGS HOPED FOR, THE CONVICTION OF THINGS NOT SEEN."

I have believed in something so big it scared me. That's called faith! Today, I choose faith. I choose to believe what my mind wants me to believe is impossible. I believe that anything is possible through God's infinite wisdom and power. I believe that my big thing is possible because God did not give me a dream that He, nor I are unable to fulfill. He gave me the dream to show me that with faith, I can achieve great things. I am believing God for bigger than big today.

I believe in God's timing, confident that His perfect timing aligns with my highest good.

ECCLESIASTES 3:1 (NASB1995)

"THERE IS AN APPOINTED TIME FOR EVERYTHING. AND THERE IS A TIME FOR EVERY EVENT UNDER HEAVEN."

There are times when I am frantically rushing out the door in the morning, frustrated because I am running late, and then I discover a car accident along the way. I remember the feeling of relief that swept over me when I saw the accident and realized that had I left the house a few moments earlier, I could have been in that accident. That is a perfect example of God's timing. There are moments in life that make us feel as though time is running out, we have missed something, or we have not achieved our goals in our designated timeframe. Yet, divine timing is rarely synchronized with man's timing. While we do not understand God's timing, it is important that we trust it and know that He always has our highest good in mind.

In every challenge, I find strength in God's presence, knowing He empowers me to overcome.

PHILIPPIANS 4:13 (ESV)

"I CAN DO ALL THINGS THROUGH HIM WHO STRENGTHENS ME."

Sometimes, I need reminders that my challenges are not happening to me; they are happening for me. I need reminders that what I see as challenges are simply lessons disguised as difficult situations. I need reminders that my perspective is everything, especially when I am facing difficult situations. Reframing a challenge as something sent to facilitate growth can help me learn the lesson that God intended. I know that while I may bend, I will not break. I was made for this.

*I am a vessel of God's love and grace,
embracing His power that flows
through me in all aspects of my life.*

2 TIMOTHY 1:9 (ESV)

"WHO SAVED US AND CALLED US TO A HOLY CALLING, NOT BECAUSE OF OUR WORKS BUT BECAUSE OF HIS OWN PURPOSE AND GRACE, WHICH HE GAVE US IN CHRIST JESUS BEFORE THE AGES BEGAN."

When God created me, He did so with a purpose. That purpose was for me to be an agent of love and grace. In my life, that looks like finding ways to be kind to a difficult co-worker. Paying for a stranger's coffee at Starbucks. Or showing grace to my children when they need it most. There are countless ways that I can demonstrate God's love and grace. He gives me multiple opportunities daily; I must be mindful of them. Each day, I will ask: How will I be a vessel of God's love and grace today?

God's love and guidance surround me, and He is paving a path for my success.

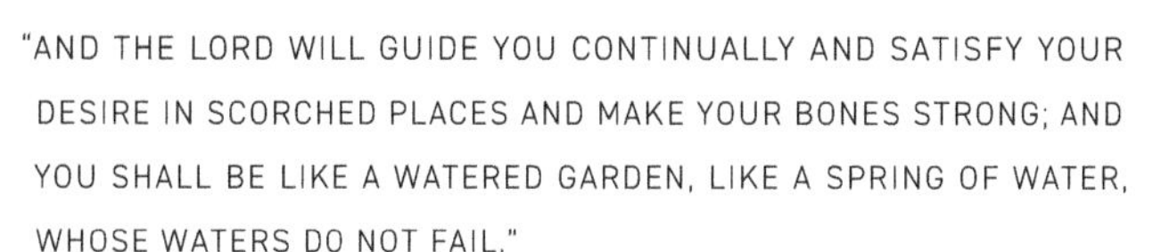

ISAIAH 58:11 (ESV)

"AND THE LORD WILL GUIDE YOU CONTINUALLY AND SATISFY YOUR DESIRE IN SCORCHED PLACES AND MAKE YOUR BONES STRONG; AND YOU SHALL BE LIKE A WATERED GARDEN, LIKE A SPRING OF WATER, WHOSE WATERS DO NOT FAIL."

I know and love that feeling of freshly laundered, crisp, warm sheets sliding against my skin as I settle in and drift asleep. I love that comforting feeling when I put on my favorite hoodie on the first day of fall. That's what God's love and guidance feels like. Warm, safe, reassuring. I also know that God's guidance feels like a parent pulling their child's arm as they scream and cry in protest. While the child does not understand the redirecting, the parent does, and thus, they do what's necessary to get the child on track and in the right direction. That is also what God's love and guidance feels like. I cherish what God's love and guidance currently look and feel like in my life.

God's infinite wisdom and power are always working on my behalf, clearing obstacles and creating opportunities.

JAMES 3:17 (NIV)

"BUT THE WISDOM THAT COMES FROM HEAVEN IS FIRST OF ALL PURE; THEN PEACE-LOVING, CONSIDERATE, SUBMISSIVE, FULL OF MERCY AND GOOD FRUIT, IMPARTIAL AND SINCERE."

When I encounter obstacles, it's normal for me to spend time and energy focusing on the obstacle. I ask myself things like, "How am I going to make it through this?" "What am I going to do now?" or, "How/why did this happen?" However, when I remember that God, in His infinite wisdom and power, sees and knows all, I am reminded that He knew this day would come in my life. He knew that I would find myself in a time of trouble or uncertainty. He also knew that this time would be a season, not a permanent state. Most importantly, He knew that on the other side of obstacles is a sea of opportunity. The opportunity to grow, to learn, and to become better and stronger than I was before. Today, I walk in God's infinite wisdom, trusting that He is always working behind the scenes to clear my path!

I release my worries to God, knowing that He is orchestrating the perfect outcomes for my growth and betterment.

1 PETER 5:6-7 (ESV)

"HUMBLE YOURSELVES, THEREFORE, UNDER THE MIGHTY HAND OF GOD SO THAT AT THE PROPER TIME HE MAY EXALT YOU, CASTING ALL YOUR ANXIETIES ON HIM, BECAUSE HE CARES FOR YOU."

It's a beautiful thing to know that I don't have to worry because I know The One who holds tomorrow in His hands. The peace that comes from knowing God and trusting that He has my best interest at heart is truly a peace like none other. Sometimes, I need reminders of this because life's circumstances can alter my vision and shake my faith. This is my reminder that God's got me. He's holding me and my loved ones in the safety of His love. I can rest in His grace. I can rest in His love. I can rest in His protection. I can rest in His favor. And when it feels as if no one cares for me, I remember that He loves and cares for me endlessly.

As I rest peacefully, I have faith that God is working behind the scenes, aligning everything for my favor and blessing.

PHILIPPIANS 4:7 (ESV)

"AND THE PEACE OF GOD, WHICH SURPASSES ALL UNDERSTANDING, WILL GUARD YOUR HEARTS AND MINDS THROUGH CHRIST JESUS."

I often exhaust myself trying to understand every detail of a situation or of my life in general. It's a normal human reaction to want to understand things. God gave me a curious nature when He created me. However, He has also called me to trust in Him and His plan for my life. When I surrender to His plan, I open myself to receive His peace which truly surpasses all understanding.

I am worthy of love and kindness, starting with myself.

COLOSSIANS 3:12 (NKJV)

"THEREFORE, AS *THE* ELECT OF GOD, HOLY AND BELOVED, PUT ON TENDER MERCIES, KINDNESS, HUMILITY, MEEKNESS, LONGSUFFERING."

I am one of God's chosen people, His elect. As His elect, He calls me to be holy and operate in ways that bring glory to Him. In doing this, I am pleasing to Him, and I am also worthy of love and kindness because I embody these characteristics. This will echo the way I treat others as well. I choose today to think, speak, and act in a way that constantly reminds me that I am worthy of love and kindness.

I embrace my imperfections, for they make me uniquely beautiful.

PSALM 139:16 (NKJV)

"YOUR EYES SAW MY SUBSTANCE, BEING YET UNFORMED. AND IN YOUR BOOK THEY ALL WERE WRITTEN, THE DAYS FASHIONED FOR ME, WHEN *AS YET THERE WERE* NONE OF THEM."

My flaws do not disqualify me from receiving God's love. My flaws and imperfections are part of my growth and development. I must realize that God loves me unconditionally and calls me to love others unconditionally as well. God knew me before I was created in my mother's womb, and He loved me then. Today, I find ways to embrace my flaws.

I prioritize my wellbeing and nurture my body, mind, and soul.

3 JOHN 1:2 (ESV)

"BELOVED, I PRAY THAT ALL MAY GO WELL WITH YOU AND THAT YOU MAY BE IN GOOD HEALTH, AS IT GOES WELL WITH YOUR SOUL."

Self-care is not selfish. In fact, it is the greatest gift that I can give to those around me. When I care for myself, I am able to show up as the best version of myself. I also model this healthy behavior to everyone around me. I consider how much more peaceful the world would be if everyone showed up as the best version of themselves and responded accordingly. Each day, I take steps to prioritize my wellbeing and self-care.

I deserve happiness and will treat myself with compassion.

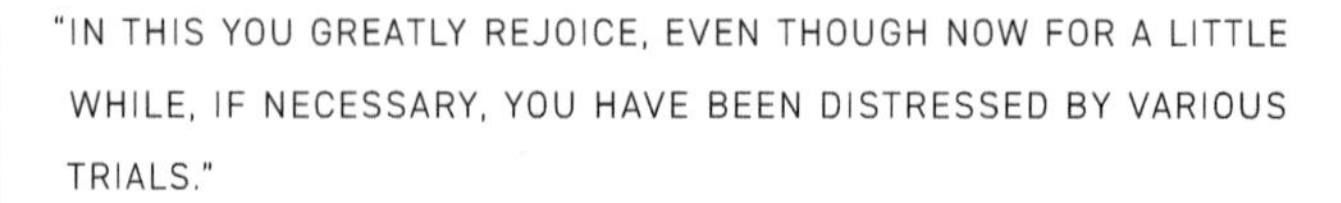

1 PETER 1:6 (NASB1995)

"IN THIS YOU GREATLY REJOICE, EVEN THOUGH NOW FOR A LITTLE WHILE, IF NECESSARY, YOU HAVE BEEN DISTRESSED BY VARIOUS TRIALS."

It is easy to be happy and feel joy when things are going well. My happiness is an inside job, and it is not dependent on external circumstances. I acknowledge that life is about seasons. I know that seasons change, therefore I will not allow my happiness to be dictated by the weather or season which will always change. However, when I understand that everything is temporary, I can easily adapt during times of difficulty and growth. I visualize what happiness looks and feels like for me. I walk in this visualization daily, ensuring that my daily thoughts, words, actions directly contribute to my overall happiness and wellbeing.

I am enough as I am, and I choose to love and accept myself completely.

PSALM 139:14 (ESV)

"I PRAISE YOU, FOR I AM FEARFULLY AND WONDERFULLY MADE. WONDERFUL ARE YOUR WORKS; MY SOUL KNOWS IT VERY WELL."

God's love is a gift that I do not have to earn. It is my birthright. It was mine when I was born, and it can never be taken from me. There is nothing I can say or do that will change God's love for me. That alone is enough for me to love myself in the same way...completely and unconditionally.

I make a major impact in the world.

1 PETER 4:10 (NASB1995)

"AS EACH ONE HAS RECEIVED A *SPECIAL* GIFT, EMPLOY IT IN SERVING ONE ANOTHER AS GOOD STEWARDS OF THE MANIFOLD GRACE OF GOD."

No one in the world has my unique gifts and talents. Sure, there may be people who are in the same field or line of work. There may be people who look similar to me. But I am one of a kind. My gifts and talents are as unique as my fingerprint. When God created me, He made me one of one. He had a specific plan for my gifts. My assignment is to figure out what that plan is and follow it accordingly. It is time for me to shine in the way that only I can.

I choose to prioritize my peace in stressful situations.

JOHN 14:27 (NIV)

"PEACE, I LEAVE WITH YOU; MY PEACE I GIVE YOU. I DO NOT GIVE TO YOU AS THE WORLD GIVES. DO NOT LET YOUR HEARTS BE TROUBLED AND DO NOT BE AFRAID."

I have been in situations that robbed me of my peace (or attempted to). When I find myself in one of these situations, I pause. I take a second to step back, take a deep breath, and think about what is important in the moment. Sometimes, all I need is to take a second to cool down and diffuse my emotions. In that moment of cooling down, I remember that God is in control. When I am in situations that are stressful, I am given the opportunity to flex my peace muscle. I remember that nothing is worth my peace. If it costs me my peace, I cannot afford it! I breathe in, breathe out... and trust that everything will be okay.

I will practice mindfulness and be fully present in each moment of this day.

MATTHEW 6:34 (NIV)

"THEREFORE, DO NOT WORRY ABOUT TOMORROW, FOR TOMORROW WILL WORRY ABOUT ITSELF. EACH DAY HAS ENOUGH TROUBLE OF ITS OWN."

To be fully present means not focusing on anything other than what is directly in front of me. When I am eating breakfast, I will savor every bite. I will slow down, take a deep breath, and chew my food. I will smile as I pay attention to the taste, texture, and temperature of my food and how delicious it is. I will think about how wonderful it is to enjoy a delicious meal that will provide my mind and body with the fuel it needs to carry me through my day. I won't worry about what's waiting for me at the office. I won't wonder what I will eat for lunch or dinner. I focus only on the meal that is directly in front of me, right now. This is how I can practice being more mindful.

Worrying about the future robs me of enjoying the beauty of the present.

I love and appreciate my body for the incredible vessel it is.

1 CORINTHIANS 6:19-20 (NIV)

"DO YOU NOT KNOW THAT YOUR BODIES ARE TEMPLES OF THE HOLY SPIRIT, WHO IS IN YOU, WHOM YOU HAVE RECEIVED FROM GOD? YOU ARE NOT YOUR OWN; YOU WERE BOUGHT AT A PRICE. THEREFORE, HONOR GOD WITH YOUR BODIES."

To love my body is to honor God. God created my body as the vehicle to carry me through this life. I show my body love and appreciation by speaking kind words to and about it. The next time I look in the mirror I will change the story I tell myself about a particular thing I normally cringe about. Instead of saying, "Oh I hate my thighs," I will say, "I love my thighs because they hold me up when I stand and they allow me to walk, run, and do the things I need to do." Adopting a healthy and loving mindset toward my body will have a positive impact on my self-esteem.

I release self-judgment and embrace self-compassion in all aspects of my life.

PSALM 145: 9 (NIV)

"THE LORD IS GOOD TO ALL; HE HAS COMPASSION ON ALL HE HAS MADE."

My relationship with myself is the one I will be in the longest. I cultivate it into one that is loving, accepting, free of judgment, and full of compassion. None of us are perfect; there is no reason to expect perfection from myself or to punish myself for making mistakes. God shows me great mercy when I make mistakes. He loves me unconditionally. I am a wonderful being with so much to offer the world. I allow myself to learn from mistakes and find ways to practice self-compassion when I fall short.

I forgive myself for past mistakes and allow myself to grow and evolve.

PSALM 92:12-14 (NIV)

"THE RIGHTEOUS WILL FLOURISH LIKE A PALM TREE, THEY WILL GROW LIKE A CEDAR OF LEBANON; PLANTED IN THE HOUSE OF THE LORD, THEY WILL FLOURISH IN THE COURTS OF OUR GOD. THEY WILL STILL BEAR FRUIT IN OLD AGE; THEY WILL STAY FRESH AND GREEN."

Forgiveness is a key component of my growth and evolution. When I know better, I do better. While it may be challenging, I will remember that I am better now than I was even yesterday. I am always growing and learning. Every experience teaches me something and thus, causes me to be better. I embrace my experiences and ask myself, "What is this teaching me, what am I supposed to learn from this?" Adapting this mindset enhances my resilience and ability to overcome adversity.

I honor my needs and set healthy boundaries to protect my emotional wellbeing.

GALATIANS 5:13 (NLT)

"FOR YOU HAVE BEEN CALLED TO LIVE IN FREEDOM, MY BROTHERS, AND SISTERS. BUT DON'T USE YOUR FREEDOM TO SATISFY YOUR SINFUL NATURE. INSTEAD, USE YOUR FREEDOM TO SERVE ONE ANOTHER IN LOVE."

Setting boundaries protects my energy because it does not allow others to act in ways that could be harmful to me. As someone who has struggled with setting boundaries in the past, this is empowering!

I am the President and CEO of my life! It is crucial that I hire and fire accordingly. I let go of relationships that are no longer serving me, and that dishonor God. Do not be readily present and available for people who are not readily present and available to me. I will start applying this to my current relationships. I will notice an improvement in my mood, stress level, and the overall satisfaction with my life.

I celebrate my achievements, no matter how big or small.

PSALM 118:24 (ESV)

"THIS IS THE DAY WHICH THE LORD HAS MADE; LET US REJOICE AND BE GLAD IN IT."

Celebrating creates positive reinforcement, which is crucial for creating habits or changing behavior. By celebrating my accomplishments, I am sending a message to my brain that this behavior is good and should be repeated. I am proud of myself for achieving something. I celebrate each accomplishment until it becomes a habit.

My best is good enough. I am enough.

PROVERBS 21:5 (NASB1995)

"THE PLANS OF THE DILIGENT *LEAD* SURELY TO ADVANTAGE, BUT EVERYONE WHO IS HASTY COMES SURELY TO POVERTY."

God loves it when I give things my best efforts. I rest assured that my best is good enough and will yield the results that I seek. Great things take time to come to fruition, but I know that every step I have taken gets me one step closer to my desired goal. God gets the glory when I apply my best in every area of my life. I choose to keep striving and moving forward. God sees me and is working in my favor with every step that I take.

I move from lesson to lesson with no loss of enthusiasm.

PSALM 119:71 (KJV)

"*IT IS* GOOD FOR ME THAT I HAVE BEEN AFFLICTED, THAT I MAY LEARN YOUR STATUTES."

Pain and failure can be my best teachers. Yet, like others, I put significant effort into avoiding them both. A wise person once told me to develop a healthy relationship with failure. I can learn from the missteps of failure and move differently the next time I see signs of it. I don't run from pain or failure; I lean into it, pulling from the knowledge they can bring. I honor the vital lessons pain and failure have taught me.

I prioritize and embrace moments of rest.

HEBREWS 4:10 (KJV)

"FOR HE THAT IS ENTERED INTO HIS REST, HE ALSO HATH CEASED FROM HIS OWN WORKS, AS GOD *DID* FROM HIS."

Rest is as important as work. Without rest, my mind, body, and soul don't have the opportunity to recharge. Severe lack of rest can lead to burnout, which can have long-lasting negative effects on my physical, mental, and emotional wellbeing. By resting on the Sabbath, God gave me the best example of how I should prioritize rest in my life.

Self-love is my foundation, and I nurture it every day.

2 CORINTHIANS 12:9 (ESV)

"BUT HE SAID TO ME, "MY GRACE IS SUFFICIENT FOR YOU, FOR MY POWER IS MADE PERFECT IN WEAKNESS." THEREFORE, I WILL BOAST ALL THE MORE GLADLY ABOUT MY WEAKNESSES, SO THAT CHRIST'S POWER MAY REST ON ME."

God wants me to look at myself through His eyes and see how beautiful I am. He didn't make any mistakes. Regardless of my flaws, shortcomings, and current situation, He sees me, and He loves me. I take a look in the mirror and remind myself that I am loved by the Most High.

I believe the promises of God for my life.

HEBREWS 10:35-36 (NIV)

"YOU NEED TO PERSEVERE SO THAT WHEN YOU HAVE DONE THE WILL OF GOD, YOU WILL RECEIVE WHAT HE HAS PROMISED."

When I am unsure of what God promised me, my goals, dreams, and God-given abilities provide helpful insight. When God made me, He instilled certain skills, desires, abilities, and talents. Those things are intimately tied to my life's calling. God knew His mission for my life when He created me. God has hidden promises for me in His Word. When I spend time in His Word, I discover those promises. I challenge myself today to read and believe the promises of God for my life.

I delight in my journey without being too focused on the destination.

1 PETER 1:18-21 (NJKV)

"KNOWING THAT YOU WERE NOT REDEEMED WITH CORRUPTIBLE THINGS, *LIKE* SILVER OR GOLD, FROM YOUR AIMLESS CONDUCT *RECEIVED* BY TRADITION FROM YOUR FATHERS, BUT WITH THE PRECIOUS BLOOD OF CHRIST, AS OF A LAMB WITHOUT BLEMISH AND WITHOUT SPOT. HE INDEED WAS FOREORDAINED BEFORE THE FOUNDATION OF THE WORLD BUT WAS MANIFEST IN THESE LAST TIMES FOR YOU WHO THROUGH HIM BELIEVE IN GOD, WHO RAISED HIM FROM THE DEAD AND GAVE HIM GLORY, SO THAT YOUR FAITH AND HOPE ARE IN GOD."

"It's about the journey, not the destination." Is this truthful for me? Definitely! While the destination is my goal and where I would like to be, there are so many valuable lessons that I learn along the way. Often, these lessons hold key clues or pieces of information that I need to reach my destination. If I miss these key pieces of information, I could miss a vital lesson needed to reach my destination. When I finally reach my destination, I will realize the importance of the journey.

I am a beacon of peace, radiating calmness and serenity.

JOHN 16:33 (ESV)

"I HAVE SAID THESE THINGS TO YOU, THAT IN ME YOU MAY HAVE PEACE. IN THE WORLD YOU WILL HAVE TRIBULATION. BUT TAKE HEART; I HAVE OVERCOME THE WORLD."

Approaching my day from a calm state of mind can be the difference between having a horrible day and having a blissful day. True peace is independent of my external circumstances. I prioritize my peace by staying centered and balanced in my most challenging moments. If one of those moments arises today, I will take a moment to close my eyes and take deep breaths. This will help me to remain calm and remember that my trust is in God, and He's got me!

I regulate my emotions and do not allow them to lead me.

PROVERBS 15:18 (ESV)

"A HOT-TEMPERED MAN STIRS UP STRIFE, BUT HE WHO IS SLOW TO ANGER QUIETS CONTENTION."

Emotions are like waves crashing and falling with the tide. Emotions are immensely powerful and can cause me to feel as if I am out of control. Learning to regulate my emotions and riding their waves is one of the ways I can achieve emotional self-mastery. In His Word, God calls me to master my emotions and not allow them to wreak havoc in my life. This is often easier said than done, but it is a skill that can be learned with practice. I will observe my emotions. I will identify them for what they are and delay taking immediate action on them. I will remind myself that I control my emotions; my emotions do not control me.

With each breath, I am becoming the best version of myself.

PHILIPPIANS 3:14 (KJV)

"I PRESS TOWARD THE MARK FOR THE PRIZE OF THE HIGH CALLING OF GOD IN CHRIST JESUS."

I was chosen for greatness. I was called to be a difference-maker in my family. My path has not been easy, but adversity births strength of character. I am determined, and I do not quit even when I want to. I may cry, I may hurt, I may bend, but I never break. I am an unstoppable force to be reckoned with. Darkness cannot remain when I enter the room; my light illuminates the darkest of nights. I am growing, learning, and becoming stronger every day. I'm proud of me. I keep marching forward. I am almost there!

Let your Life be affirmed

February:

Divine Timing and God's Plan

Trusting God, The Process, and The Plan

When I think about divine timing, I process it through the lens of baking a cake. You preheat the oven, assemble the necessary ingredients, combine them, place the mixture in the oven, and you wait. God's timing and plan for our lives is much like this. He allows us to experience certain situations to teach us certain things; this can be much like the process of assembling the ingredients. He needs us to learn and understand certain things to get us where He needs us to be. Every lesson that we learn is adding one more necessary ingredient to our cake.

As we travel along our path, we may not realize it, but God is carefully combining the ingredients and preparing us. If you've lived long enough, you know that some situations most certainly feel like we are being baked in an oven, right? The pressure and the heat do not feel good – but they are helping us to achieve a beautiful outcome.

As you begin this month, focus on God's divine timing and plan for your life. I know it's not always easy and I know that being in the oven of life's trials and tribulations can sometimes bring you to your knees. But I also know how delicious the cake is once it's finished baking. You've still baking, sis. Allow God's timing and process to perfect His Word within you.

I trust in the divine plan for my life, knowing that God's guidance leads me to where I need to be. I know that He is opening doors for me even when I cannot see them.

ROMANS 8:28 (ESV)

"AND WE KNOW THAT FOR THOSE WHO LOVE GOD ALL THINGS WORK TOGETHER FOR GOOD, FOR THOSE WHO ARE CALLED ACCORDING TO HIS PURPOSE."

I often find myself worrying and wondering about what tomorrow will bring. I exert energy trying to anticipate a specific outcome. This is my sign to rest in and on the Word of God, which tells me that the divine plan is for my greatest good. I rest and trust in the promises of God and watch His plan unfold in my life.

I work diligently on my craft as I wait patiently for the promises of God to manifest in my life.

HEBREWS 6:15 (NLV)

"ABRAHAM WAS WILLING TO WAIT AND GOD GAVE TO HIM WHAT HE HAD PROMISED."

It takes 10,000 hours to master a skill. Each day is an opportunity to get closer to my 10,000. With every hour of practice, I am learning and gaining more knowledge and experience. While I often find myself waiting on God, He calls me to work as I wait. I am dedicated to working while I am waiting. The lifestyle that I desire is intricately intertwined with my effort and patience. I know that God's timing is perfect, and I align myself with his will and purpose for my life!

I am capable of handling whatever comes my way.

JAMES 1:12 (ESV)

"BLESSED IS THE MAN WHO REMAINS STEADFAST UNDER TRIAL, FOR WHEN HE HAS STOOD THE TEST HE WILL RECEIVE THE CROWN OF LIFE, WHICH GOD HAS PROMISED TO THOSE WHO LOVE HIM."

I got this. I am the chosen one for the job. My doubts and fears do not define me. I am powerful beyond measure. I am courageous. I am strong. I remain calm under pressure, allowing insightful solutions to various problems that arise. I am a fierce and mighty prayer warrior, and that is one of my greatest strengths. I am beyond capable. I was built for this. I know who I am. I adjust my crown and stand tall. I've got this!

I choose to celebrate progress over perfection.

1 CORINTHIANS 15:58 (NKJV)

"THEREFORE, MY BELOVED BROTHERS, BE STEADFAST, IMMOVABLE, ALWAYS ABOUNDING IN THE WORK OF THE LORD, KNOWING THAT IN THE LORD YOUR LABOR IS NOT IN VAIN."

No one will ever be perfect. Perfectionism can be toxic and counterproductive, not to mention unrealistic. Progress, however, is very realistic and attainable. Committing to small daily changes will result in the formation of new habits. I commit to doing better today. And the day after that. I will keep putting one foot in front of the other. I can do it!

I trust in my God-given ability to find solutions and overcome challenges.

ISAIAH 41:13 (NIV)

"FOR I AM THE LORD, YOUR GOD, WHO TAKES HOLD OF YOUR RIGHT HAND AND SAYS TO YOU, DO NOT FEAR; I WILL HELP YOU."

Challenges do not announce themselves in advance or wait for a convenient time. In fact, there is never really a convenient time to face a challenge. I choose to change my relationship with challenges. I choose to consider them as opportunities for my growth and betterment. I acknowledge that there is a correlation between my biggest challenges and my greatest lessons. Whatever challenges I am currently facing, I know that I am more than capable of facing them head-on. I am bold, brave, and courageous. I do not back down or cower in the face of adversity. I step up and rise to the occasion every time. I am a warrior and a queen! I will overcome. I am victorious.

I release the need to control everything and embrace the flow of life.

JAMES 1:6 (NIV)

"BUT WHEN YOU ASK, YOU MUST BELIEVE AND NOT DOUBT, BECAUSE THE ONE WHO DOUBTS IS LIKE A WAVE OF THE SEA, BLOWN AND TOSSED BY THE WIND."

There is a beautiful ease and sense of peace that comes with letting go and letting it flow. Having a need to control everything is like trying to hold onto a slippery bar of soap. The tighter I hold on, the more it slips away. If I loosen my grip, I will find that the bar of soap rests in my hand. I apply this approach to my life; and I no longer grip so tightly to situations that are outside of my control. Living in the peace and divine flow of God's will is a beautiful thing, and I deserve it!

I believe in myself and my abilities; I have the strength to succeed.

LUKE 12:48 (ESV)

"BUT THE ONE WHO DID NOT KNOW, AND DID WHAT DESERVED A BEATING, WILL RECEIVE A LIGHT BEATING. EVERYONE TO WHOM MUCH WAS GIVEN, OF HIM MUCH WILL BE REQUIRED, AND FROM HIM TO WHOM THEY ENTRUSTED MUCH, THEY WILL DEMAND THE MORE."

I am brilliant. I am special. I am important. My superpower is that there is only one of me. My unique skills and abilities are my launching pad for my wildest dreams. My dream lifestyle lies on the other side of my belief in myself. I can accomplish anything that I put my mind to. This is my daily reminder to walk in my greatness. I know that God has given me gifts and abilities that will positively impact lives. There is no room for self-doubt on my path to success!

Every step forward, no matter how small, brings me closer to my goals.

MATTHEW 25:21 (ESV)

"HIS MASTER SAID TO HIM, 'WELL DONE, GOOD AND FAITHFUL SERVANT. YOU HAVE BEEN FAITHFUL OVER A LITTLE; I WILL SET YOU OVER MUCH. ENTER INTO THE JOY OF YOUR MASTER.'"

I am so proud of my efforts. I am trying hard. I am doing the work. I am making sacrifices. I am studying my craft. I am setting a powerful and positive example for everyone around me. It's a beautiful thing to see! I am focused and putting one foot in front of the other. My dedication will yield the results that I am looking for. I will stay the course. I will encourage myself. I will remember that I am capable.

I embrace mistakes as learning opportunities, I grow stronger from them.

2 PETER 3:9 (NLT)

"THE LORD ISN'T REALLY BEING SLOW ABOUT HIS PROMISE, AS SOME PEOPLE THINK. NO, HE IS BEING PATIENT FOR MY SAKE. HE DOES NOT WANT ANYONE TO BE DESTROYED, BUT WANTS EVERYONE TO REPENT."

Embracing mistakes is the key to unlocking my full potential and achieving greatness. Every stumble, every setback, and every wrong turn is not a sign of failure but a steppingstone towards success. It's through these missteps that I learn, grow, and evolve into the best version of myself. Mistakes are the catalyst for innovation and fuel for resilience. They are the chapters in the book of my life that make the story worth telling. So, I don't fear mistakes. I welcome them with open arms. I embrace them as opportunities to learn, adapt, and ultimately, to soar higher than I ever thought possible. I remember, the most beautiful flowers often grow from the deepest, richest soils, and so do I.

My resilience and determination are leading me to achieve great things.

ISAIAH 40:31 (KJV)

"BUT THEY THAT WAIT UPON THE LORD SHALL RENEW THEIR STRENGTH; THEY SHALL MOUNT UP WITH WINGS AS EAGLES, THEY SHALL RUN AND NOT BE WEARY, AND THEY SHALL WALK AND NOT FAINT."

Resilience and determination are the twin pillars that support the pathway to achieving great things. When faced with adversity, it's not the strongest or the most talented who prevail but those who refuse to give up. It's the belief in my dreams and the relentless pursuit of my goals that set me apart.

I admit the road to success is often filled with potholes, but it's my resilience that turns those stumbling blocks into strengths. So, when challenges arise, I embrace them as opportunities to showcase my determination and relentless faith in God.

I know that every setback is a setup for a comeback, and with persistence, I can accomplish things that once seemed impossible. My story of triumph will inspire others to reach for their own greatness, proving that with resilience and determination, the sky is not the limit – it's the beginning. I am rooting for myself! I am flying high!

God's promises are unshakeable, and He will fulfill them in His perfect timing.

HABAKKUK 2:3 (NIV)

"FOR THE REVELATION AWAITS AN APPOINTED TIME; IT SPEAKS OF THE END AND WILL NOT PROVE FALSE. THOUGH IT LINGER, WAIT FOR IT; IT WILL CERTAINLY COME AND WILL NOT DELAY."

My faith is a source of strength and a testament to God's unwavering love and faithfulness. Even when it seems like my dreams and prayers are taking longer to materialize than I'd like, I must remember that His timing is always perfect. It's in the waiting that I grow, learn patience, and develop the trust needed to fully embrace His blessings when they arrive. So, I keep my faith strong, trust in His plan, and know that every promise He has made to me will be fulfilled in His divine and perfect timing. One day, I will be living in my answered prayers.

No one can hinder the blessings God has in store for me.

JEREMIAH 17:7 (ESV)

"BLESSED IS THE MAN WHO TRUSTS IN THE LORD, AND WHOSE TRUST IS THE LORD."

God's love and grace are endless, and His plans for my life are filled with hope and prosperity. Regardless of the challenges, obstacles, or negativity that may arise, I find solace in knowing that God's purpose prevails. The path He has set before me is uniquely mine, and no human limitation can deter the blessings He intends to pour into my life. With unwavering faith and a heart full of gratitude, I walk confidently, knowing that His favor surrounds me, and His blessings will flow abundantly in His perfect time.

I am confident that God's favor and grace will prevail in every aspect of my life.

2 CORINTHIANS 12:9 (NIV)

"BUT HE SAID TO ME, "MY GRACE IS SUFFICIENT FOR YOU, FOR MY POWER IS MADE PERFECT IN WEAKNESS." THEREFORE, I WILL BOAST EVEN MORE GLADLY ABOUT MY WEAKNESSES, SO THAT CHRIST'S POWER MAY REST ON ME."

God's grace is a constant source of strength, and it knows no limits. With faith the size of a mustard seed, I embrace each day with the confidence that His hand is guiding my path, His wisdom is illuminating my decisions, and His favor is opening doors that no one can shut. No challenge is too great, and no circumstance is too daunting when I walk hand in hand with the Almighty. In every endeavor, I am assured that His favor will shine upon me, His grace will sustain me, and His blessings will overflow in abundance.

Love is God's greatest gift. I lead with love in all aspects of my life.

JOHN 3:16 (BLB)

"FOR GOD SO LOVED THE WORLD THAT HE GAVE HIS ONLY BEGOTTEN SON, THAT EVERYONE BELIEVING IN HIM SHOULD NOT PERISH, BUT SHOULD HAVE ETERNAL LIFE."

One of my greatest responsibilities as a believer in Christ is to lead with love. Love is deeply woven into the tapestry of my words, thoughts, and actions. Because of His love, I am saved. Because of His love, I am enough. Because of His love, I have been redeemed. Because of His love, I can overcome and be great. God's love is always with me. When I feel I don't deserve it, He still loves me. When I stumble and fall, He still loves me. There is nothing I can do that will cause Him to stop loving me. I am blessed simply because He loves me.

I trust that God's power is greater than any challenges I may face, and He will see me through.

MATTHEW 19:26 (ESV)

"BUT JESUS LOOKED AT THEM AND SAID, "WITH MAN THIS IS IMPOSSIBLE, BUT WITH GOD ALL THINGS ARE POSSIBLE."

The power of God is a force beyond measure, an omnipotent presence that shapes the universe and breathes life into every soul. It's in His power that I find hope when I am lost, strength when I am weary, and healing when I am broken. His love knows no bounds, and His mercy is endless.

In times of despair, His power lifts me from the depths of darkness and sets my feet upon solid ground. It's a power that transforms lives, redeems the lost, and offers grace to the undeserving. In His presence, I discover the true essence of strength and the boundless potential of faith.

When I embrace the power of God, I find that there is no challenge too great, no obstacle too insurmountable, for in Him, all things are possible. With Him, I can declare victory!

My determination, work ethic, and God-given talents and gifts will lead me to success and prosperity.

1 KINGS 2:3 (NIV)

"...AND OBSERVE WHAT THE LORD YOUR GOD REQUIRES: WALK IN OBEDIENCE TO HIM, AND KEEP HIS DECREES AND COMMANDS, HIS LAWS AND REGULATIONS, AS WRITTEN IN THE LAW OF MOSES. DO THIS SO THAT I MAY PROSPER IN ALL YOU DO AND WHEREVER YOU GO."

True prosperity is the beautiful woven patterns of hard work, determination, and the God-given talents that reside within me. When I align my efforts with the gifts God has bestowed upon me, remarkable things happen! It's not merely about material wealth but about flourishing in every aspect of my life—spiritually, emotionally, and physically.

Through diligent labor and faith, I unlock the doors to success, allowing God's blessings to flow freely in my life. It's the harmony of my efforts with His divine plan that brings about the truest form of prosperity—a life lived in purpose, abundance, and service to others.

I am proud of my talents. I work tirelessly and trust in His guidance, for in this synergy, prosperity becomes a testament to His grace and the potential for greatness that resides within me and has resided in me all along.

God's hand is upon me, protecting and guiding me through life's journey.

PSALM 56:3-4 (KJV)

"WHAT TIME I AM AFRAID, I WILL TRUST IN THEE. IN GOD I WILL PRAISE HIS WORD, IN GOD I HAVE PUT MY TRUST; I WILL NOT FEAR WHAT FLESH CAN DO UNTO ME."

As I journey through life, I can find solace and strength in the knowledge of God's protection and guidance. This protection is so seamless that I don't even notice it. His love is a steadfast shield that shields me from harm. His wisdom is the guiding light that leads me through even the darkest of times.

In God's hands, I am not merely a survivor; I am a conqueror, able to weather any storm and prevail over any obstacle. I trust in His protection and follow His guidance, knowing that my path is illuminated, my purpose is clear, and my spirit is fortified with an unbreakable faith that propels me toward a future filled with hope, grace, and blessings.

God's presence in my life brings strength and courage to overcome any adversity.

JOSHUA 1:9 (NIV)

"HAVE I NOT COMMANDED YOU? BE STRONG AND COURAGEOUS. DO NOT BE AFRAID; DO NOT BE DISCOURAGED, FOR THE LORD YOUR GOD WILL BE WITH YOU WHEREVER YOU GO."

The presence of God in my life is an endless source of strength and courage that empowers me to triumph over adversity. His divine presence fills me with a profound assurance that I am not alone in my struggles.

With the strength of God propelling me forward, my fears diminish, and my doubts fade, replaced by a steadfast belief that I can conquer any challenge. It's through the awareness of His presence that I find the resilience to endure, the wisdom to navigate, and the bravery to face adversity head-on.

In His presence, I discover an unshakeable resolve, knowing that I am equipped with His strength to conquer the storms and emerge from trials stronger, wiser, and more resilient than ever before. With God's presence, there is no obstacle too daunting, no setback too severe, for He is my refuge and the Source of courage that propels me to victory. He is with me! He is in me! He is for me! I will prevail!

I trust God's plan because I know that He loves me.

PROVERBS 16:9 (ESV)

"THE HEART OF MAN PLANS HIS WAY, BUT THE LORD ESTABLISHES HIS STEPS."

God's plan for me is a masterpiece in the making! He created it with purpose and divine intention. Every twist and turn in my life, every challenge, every triumph, and every disappointment, heartbreak, or betrayal plays a unique role in His grand design. Even when I cannot see the bigger picture, I can trust in His plan for me.

Embracing God's plan means surrendering to His guidance, acknowledging that His timing is perfect, and believing that every step I take is part of a greater journey. It is all for my greatest good!

It's in this trust that I find true peace and purpose as I contribute my unique thread to the intricate design of His masterwork, knowing that each day holds a piece of His beautiful plan waiting to be unveiled.

Nothing can thwart God's purpose for my life, and I am secure in His unwavering love and provision.

PHILIPPIANS 4:19 (ESV)

"AND MY GOD WILL SUPPLY EVERY NEED OF YOURS ACCORDING TO HIS RICHES IN GLORY IN CHRIST JESUS."

In every season, God's provision flows like a never-ending stream, meeting my needs with perfect timing and in ways I could never have imagined! I ever find myself laughing and smiling at how God has come through for me. Yet, I still worry as if He has never made a way. I am reminded I am not alone on my journey and that even amid uncertainty, I can always rely on His faithfulness.

By trusting in His provision, I release my worries and embrace a life filled with gratitude and contentment, knowing that His love will sustain me through every challenge. He will lead me to a place of abundance, spiritually and materially.

I have a healthy relationship with negativity. I understand that life is not linear, and I make space for unpleasant emotions, knowing they are part of my journey.

HEBREWS 12:7 (NIV)

"ENDURE HARDSHIP AS DISCIPLINE; GOD IS TREATING YOU AS HIS CHILDREN. FOR WHAT CHILDREN ARE NOT DISCIPLINED BY THEIR FATHER?"

Just as a skilled gardener knows that storms and rain are essential for the growth of a garden, unpleasant emotions are vital for my personal growth. I make space for them, acknowledging that they are not roadblocks but rather steppingstones along my path.

In my darkest moments, I lean on my faith and trust that God has a purpose even amid discomfort. Through resilience and a positive mindset, I find strength in adversity and transform challenges into opportunities for spiritual and personal development.

I forgive others to free myself from resentment.

COLOSSIANS 3:13 (ESV)

"BEARING WITH ONE ANOTHER AND, IF ONE HAS A COMPLAINT AGAINST ANOTHER, FORGIVING EACH OTHER; AS THE LORD HAS FORGIVEN YOU, SO YOU ALSO MUST FORGIVE."

The power of forgiveness is an extraordinary force that flows from the heart of my faith. Forgiveness is not just a gift I offer to others; it's a gift I give to myself. Harboring unforgiveness, as the saying goes, is like drinking poison but expecting the other person to die. I choose forgiveness.

When I choose to forgive, I release the heavy burden of resentment and bitterness, allowing God's grace to heal my wounds. It's a testament to the limitless love and mercy of my Heavenly Father, who forgives me in my imperfection.

Forgiveness mends relationships, restores inner peace, and paves the way for reconciliation and renewal. In embracing the power of forgiveness, I mirror Christ's example and experience a profound freedom that transcends the pain of the past, ushering me into a future filled with love, compassion, and the unshakeable peace that only God can provide.

I am in tune with the voice of God, careful to pay attention to His gentle nudges.

HEBREWS 4:12 (ESV)

"FOR THE WORD OF GOD IS LIVING AND ACTIVE, SHARPER THAN ANY TWO-EDGED SWORD, PIERCING TO THE DIVISION OF SOUL AND OF SPIRIT, OF JOINTS AND OF MARROW, AND DISCERNING THE THOUGHTS AND INTENTIONS OF THE HEART."

Today, God is challenging me to be intentional in my pursuit of His presence and to be keenly aware of His gentle nudges that are always guiding my steps.

In the stillness of prayer and reflection, I find the wisdom and clarity to discern His divine guidance amidst life's noise and distractions. With a heart attuned to His loving whispers, I trust in His perfect plan and timing, knowing that His direction leads to a life filled with purpose, peace, and blessings.

I cultivate this sacred connection, for in it, I discover the profound joy of walking with my Creator, every day, affirming His presence and purpose in my life.

I control the things I can, I release worrying about the things that I can't.

MATTHEW 6:25-26 (NIV)

"THEREFORE, I TELL YOU, DO NOT WORRY ABOUT YOUR LIFE, WHAT YOU WILL EAT OR DRINK; OR ABOUT YOUR BODY, WHAT YOU WILL WEAR. IS NOT LIFE MORE THAN FOOD, AND THE BODY MORE THAN CLOTHES?

Look at the birds of the air; they do not sow or reap or store away in barns, and yet your heavenly Father feeds them. Are you not much more valuable than they?"

Worrying about something is synonymous with praying for the things I don't want to happen. When I release the unknown to God's infinite power, I free my mind of racing thoughts and fear. This wisdom is rooted in faith and trust in God's divine plan.

While I diligently work towards my goals and aspirations, I understand that there are aspects of life beyond my control. Instead of dwelling on the uncontrollable, I choose to focus my energy on nurturing a positive mindset, maintaining resilience, and nurturing my relationship with God.

By surrendering the burdens of worry, I open the door to peace, joy, and an unbreakable faith in God's provision and guidance. Find freedom in releasing the weight of the unknown and find solace in trusting God's perfect plan.

I seek God's face and I am careful to ensure that my thoughts, words, and actions are in alignment with His will.

ROMANS 12:2 (ESV)

"DO NOT BE CONFORMED TO THIS WORLD, BUT BE TRANSFORMED BY THE RENEWAL OF YOUR MIND, THAT BY TESTING YOU MAY DISCERN WHAT IS THE WILL OF GOD, WHAT IS GOOD AND ACCEPTABLE AND PERFECT."

By surrendering my desires to His guidance daily, I can find clarity, wisdom, and God's peace that transcends understanding.

In seeking God's face and walking in His will, I unlock the transformative power of faith and align myself with the abundant blessings He has in store for me. This daily practice reminds me that my life is a testament to His grace, and every step I take is a testament to my devotion to a higher purpose.

God's plan and timing are perfect.

PSALM 27:14 (NIV)

"WAIT FOR THE LORD; BE STRONG AND TAKE HEART AND WAIT FOR THE LORD."

I have tried to tell children or younger relatives some things but realize they don't understand because they are young, and the information I was relaying to them was beyond their comprehension. This is a great way to think about God's timing and plan for my life. He is a loving parent. While He doesn't explain every detail, He leaves me clues and provides me with gentle nudges and glimpses. However, because I am often like a child, I cannot understand His moves. The blessing is that I don't have to understand. All I must do is stay on course and follow His plan for me, knowing that He loves me and has my best interest at heart.

I don't allow my sight to distract my faith in God's promises for my life.

2 CORINTHIANS 5:7 (NIV)

"FOR WE LIVE BY FAITH, NOT BY SIGHT."

Walking by faith requires me to completely surrender and believe despite what I see.

Faith is the bridge between the visible and the invisible, the tangible and the intangible. When circumstances seem bleak, I remember that God's promises are unwavering, and His plans are beyond comprehension. I choose to see through the eyes of faith, focusing on His truth and unfailing love, even when the world presents challenges and doubts.

This affirmation serves as a critical reminder to keep my gaze on God's promises. Then, I can overcome any obstacle and step confidently into the abundant life He has prepared for me. My faith is the catalyst for the miraculous, allowing me to walk in the light of His promises, even when I can't see the full picture.

God's vision requires the best version of myself. I put in the work to be the best version of myself every day.

PROVERBS 29:18 (ESV)

"WHERE THERE IS NO PROPHETIC VISION, THE PEOPLE CAST OFF RESTRAINT, BUT BLESSED IS HE WHO KEEPS THE LAW."

To fulfill God's purpose, continually strive for growth, improvement, and self-refinement. It's a daily commitment to become more compassionate, more resilient, and more faithful. By putting in the work to be the best version of myself, I align my life with His divine plan, allowing His vision to manifest through my actions and choices.

I am capable of greatness. I am evolving and becoming a vessel for His purpose, realizing that my potential is limitless when I commit to daily self-improvement guided by faith.

I walk in the essence of what God has for me, even if it hasn't manifested yet.

ROMANS 4:17 (NIV)

"AS IT IS WRITTEN: "I HAVE MADE YOU A FATHER OF MANY NATIONS." HE IS OUR FATHER IN THE SIGHT OF GOD, IN WHOM HE BELIEVED—THE GOD WHO GIVES LIFE TO THE DEAD AND CALLS INTO BEING THINGS THAT WERE NOT."

God's promises often require patience and unwavering faith. When walking in the essence of His plan, I align my actions, thoughts, and beliefs with His divine purpose, trusting that His timing is perfect. This affirmation encourages me to live with anticipation and conviction, knowing that His blessings are on the horizon. It's a reminder that my faith is not contingent on immediate results but on the assurance that God's promises will come to fruition in His perfect time. I can find fulfillment in the journey itself, for as I walk in the essence of His plan, I embrace His grace, wisdom, and love every step of the way.

Let your Life be affirmed

March:

Physical Health and Wellbeing

Mastering Your Physical Wellness

Our bodies are the vehicles that God has given us to carry us through our human experience. To operate at our best and bring Him glory, we must be at our physical best. God's Word calls us to be mindful of our diet. This is not just the food that we eat, but everything that we consume: TV shows and movies, books and social media posts, conversations we engage in, even the thoughts we think.

Keeping in mind that we thrive when we approach our health from a holistic standpoint, we must also be aware of how these things impact us. If you eat a perfectly clean and healthy diet but have toxic relationships in your life, the toxicity will negatively impact you.

This month, challenge yourself to eliminate things and/or people that are taking away from your overall wellbeing. God wants the best for you in every aspect of your life. It starts with you. I pray that this month's affirmations empower you to be your best self and help you focus on your physical and mental health.

I make conscious food choices that fuel my body for my daily activities.

1 CORINTHIANS 6:12 (NIV)

"'I HAVE THE RIGHT TO DO ANYTHING,' YOU SAY—BUT NOT EVERYTHING IS BENEFICIAL. 'I HAVE THE RIGHT TO DO ANYTHING'—BUT I WILL NOT BE MASTERED BY ANYTHING."

My body is the temple of the Holy Spirit, deserving of love and care. By mindfully selecting nourishing foods, I honor God's gift of life and vitality. My physical wellbeing is intrinsically linked to my spiritual and mental health. I prioritize nutritious choices that create energy for daily tasks but also create a harmonious balance that empowers me to live with purpose and serve others with love and vitality. The body is an instrument through which I can fulfill my calling, and by making conscious food choices, I honor God's design for my wellbeing, allowing me to be at my best for His glory.

I commit to moving my body for at least 30 minutes every day.

1 TIMOTHY 4:8 (NIV)

"FOR PHYSICAL TRAINING IS OF SOME VALUE, BUT GODLINESS HAS VALUE FOR ALL THINGS, HOLDING PROMISE FOR BOTH THE PRESENT LIFE AND THE LIFE TO COME."

My physical health is a precious gift from God, and by nurturing it, I honor myself as His creation. Daily movement isn't just about physical fitness; it's an act of stewardship for the temple He has entrusted to me. In those 30 minutes, God gives me the opportunity to clear my mind, reduce stress, and renew my spirit. It's a sacred time when I can reflect on His blessings, pray, and draw closer to Him in the beauty of His creation. By making this commitment, I not only strengthen my body but also create a space for God's presence in my daily life, allowing me to be a source of inspiration and motivation for others on their journey toward holistic wellbeing.

I find healthy ways to nourish my body when I am at social events or out to eat with friends and family.

1 PETER 5:8 (KJV)

"BE SOBER, BE VIGILANT; BECAUSE YOUR ADVERSARY THE DEVIL, AS A ROARING LION, WALKETH ABOUT, SEEKING WHOM HE MAY DEVOUR."

I seek to strike a balance between enjoying the company of loved ones and making mindful choices that honor my wellbeing. I can savor the joy of togetherness without compromising my commitment to a healthy lifestyle. Finding healthy ways to nourish the body not only maintains physical health but also shows that I can celebrate life's moments while respecting the temple God has provided me.

I do not allow negative situations to impact my food choices.

1 CORINTHIANS 10:31 (NIV)

"SO WHETHER YOU EAT OR DRINK OR WHATEVER YOU DO, DO IT ALL FOR THE GLORY OF GOD."

Food is a gift from God meant to nourish my body and provide sustenance. When faced with stress or emotional challenges, I turn to prayer and mindfulness, seeking solace and strength in God rather than the comfort of unhealthy eating habits. This will allow me to maintain a harmonious relationship with food, viewing it as a tool for nourishment rather than as a means of escape.

I prioritize a balanced approach to eating and honor God's design for my physical wellness. I inspire others to do the same. In these choices, I will find not only physical health but also spiritual and emotional balance, ultimately living in alignment with His divine purpose for my life.

I make the time to prepare nutritious and delicious meals for me and my family.

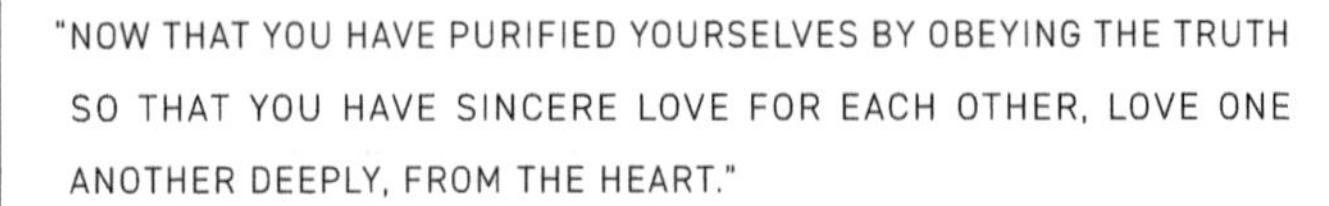

1 PETER 1:22 (NIV)

"NOW THAT YOU HAVE PURIFIED YOURSELVES BY OBEYING THE TRUTH SO THAT YOU HAVE SINCERE LOVE FOR EACH OTHER, LOVE ONE ANOTHER DEEPLY, FROM THE HEART."

The pace of life is faster, busier, and more hectic now than it has ever been. With drive-thru restaurants on every corner and hundreds of convenient food choices at my fingertips, the hustle and bustle of modern culture and society have made it challenging to prioritize preparing home-cooked meals.

Regardless of my schedule, I will find ways to make more time for home-cooked meals and snacks. I will turn it into a fun activity to enhance family bonding and practice healthy habits together. I will choose a day of the week to come together as a family and prepare batch meals that will last 3-5 days. I will be creative, have fun, and allow each member of the family to take turns choosing the meal(s) for the week.

Healthy meal planning for the family does not have to be stressful or complicated. By implementing these easy tips, my family and I can work together to make healthier food choices.

My healthy choices have a radical positive impact on everyone around me.

2 CORINTHIANS 5:9-10 (ESV)

"SO WHETHER WE ARE AT HOME OR AWAY, WE MAKE IT OUR AIM TO PLEASE HIM. FOR WE MUST ALL APPEAR BEFORE THE JUDGMENT SEAT OF CHRIST, SO THAT EACH ONE MAY RECEIVE WHAT IS DUE FOR WHAT HE HAS DONE IN THE BODY, WHETHER GOOD OR EVIL."

My choices create waves of effect. When I decide to make healthy choices, I become healthier. The people in my sphere of influence will not only take notice but they will also be influenced to do the same. Knowing that my choices affect those around me adds a level of accountability and motivation to choose well.

I am affirming this at this moment for a reason. God has tasked me with being the leader amongst my family and friends. It starts with me. I believe in me!

I prioritize exercise, and I look forward to moving my body in fun and challenging ways.

PROVERBS 27:17 (NIV)

"IRON SHARPENS IRON, AND ONE MAN SHARPENS ANOTHER."

Challenging myself to try new exercises and achieve new strength goals is one of the most fulfilling and rewarding experiences! While it is human nature to shy away from discomfort, our greatest growth can arise from it. This is especially true pertaining to physical exercise.

With every workout, I strive to push myself just a little further than I did the last time. Most of all, I make it fun! If I don't want to run, I'll dance instead! I will move my body today!

I exercise as a celebration of what my body can do, not as punishment for what I ate.

PHILIPPIANS 3:21 (ESV)

"WHO WILL TRANSFORM OUR LOWLY BODY TO BE LIKE HIS GLORIOUS BODY, BY THE POWER THAT ENABLES HIM EVEN TO SUBJECT ALL THINGS TO HIMSELF."

Rather than viewing exercise as a means of punishment for indulgences, I view it as a joyful celebration of the incredible gift that is my body! My body is capable of amazing things! I marvel at its strength, endurance, and resilience, all of which are blessings from God.

I am a spiritual being having a human experience. With each workout, I honor the Creator by nurturing the temple He has placed me in. I approach fitness with gratitude and reverence. By embracing this affirmation, I inspire others to view exercise as an act of self-love and appreciation for the incredible capabilities of the body, fostering a positive and uplifting approach to health and wellbeing.

I have a healthy relationship with food, and I exercise restraint and portion control with ease.

PROVERBS 12:1 (NIV)

"WHOEVER LOVES DISCIPLINE LOVES KNOWLEDGE, BUT WHOEVER HATES CORRECTION LACKS WISDOM."

I believe that one of the best ways to have a healthy relationship with food is to practice intuitive eating. Intuitive or mindful eating is a concept that focuses on being in tune with my body's natural hunger and fullness cues. Sometimes, I engage in mindless eating. This happens when I am stressed, emotional, or distracted while eating. By slowing down and focusing on how I feel while I am eating, I can become more skilled at letting my body tell me when it has had enough. With practice, this can become second nature. I will commit to developing a healthy relationship with food and being conscious about the food choices I make, starting now.

I understand the connection between inflammation in my mind and body; therefore, I choose foods that do not contribute to inflammation.

GENESIS 1:29 (ESV)

"AND GOD SAID, "BEHOLD, I HAVE GIVEN YOU EVERY PLANT YIELDING SEED THAT IS ON THE FACE OF ALL THE EARTH, AND EVERY TREE WITH SEED IN ITS FRUIT. YOU SHALL HAVE THEM FOR FOOD."

Inflammation can negatively impact how we feel, both physically and emotionally. Foods that are organic and unprocessed are weapons against inflammation. I challenge myself to take note of how I feel when I eat something that is not healthy.

I will pay special attention to my energy level, digestion, the time between when I eat and when I feel hungry again, and my overall mood. I will make note of these same factors after consuming a healthy meal. When I spot the difference, I will start to understand the connection between what I eat and my overall health.

This affirmation empowers me to make the choices that will help me to operate at my best every day! I believe in me!

I make the conscious decision to reverse generations of health problems with the daily food that I fuel my body with.

EXODUS 20:5-6 (NIV)

"YOU SHALL NOT BOW DOWN TO THEM OR WORSHIP THEM; FOR I, THE LORD YOUR GOD, AM A JEALOUS GOD, PUNISHING THE CHILDREN FOR THE SIN OF THE PARENTS TO THE THIRD AND FOURTH GENERATION OF THOSE WHO HATE ME, BUT SHOWING LOVE TO A THOUSAND GENERATIONS OF THOSE WHO LOVE ME AND KEEP MY COMMANDMENTS."

I have the power to change my food choices, starting today!

I choose foods that fuel me and make me feel energized. My body is the best litmus test for what foods are best for me. I pay more attention to how I feel after eating by using a food journal. I will also eliminate foods that leave me feeling sluggish or that cause digestive issues. I choose to replace them with foods that leave me feeling satisfied and light on my feet! My physical health is a crucial component to me operating at my best every day. I commit to a healthier, stronger me, and I model this behavior for my family members as well.

I am grateful for every stretch mark, pocket of fat, dimple, scar, and imperfection on my body.

1 PETER 3:8 (NIV)

"FINALLY, ALL OF YOU, BE LIKE-MINDED, BE SYMPATHETIC, LOVE ONE ANOTHER, BE COMPASSIONATE AND HUMBLE."

Sometimes, we focus too much on looking perfect. This can cause us to pick ourselves apart and dislike what we see when we look in the mirror. I must remember that God created me. When He looks at me, He sees my beauty. He sees my flaws and still thinks that I am beautiful. I should look at myself the same way. I am beautiful, flaws and all.

I only use positive words when speaking about my body.

PROVERBS 18:21 (NIV)

"THE TONGUE HAS THE POWER OF LIFE AND DEATH, AND THOSE WHO LOVE IT WILL EAT ITS FRUIT."

I speak about my body as if I am speaking about someone I love and care for deeply. Speaking negatively about my body puts negative energy into my body and into the universe.

My body is beautiful. My body is strong. My body is healthy. My body has carried me through every day of my life, and that is a blessing.

I am on a health and fitness journey, actively working to change things about my body, knowing that it is okay to want to change or improve things about my body. I commit to being kind to myself in the process. When I speak positively about my body, I subconsciously start standing taller and feeling better about myself. I will practice doing this daily, especially when I catch myself speaking negatively about my body.

I work on improving my body, not complaining about what I dislike about it.

COLOSSIANS 4:6 (ESV)

"LET YOUR SPEECH ALWAYS BE GRACIOUS, SEASONED WITH SALT, SO THAT YOU MAY KNOW HOW YOU OUGHT TO ANSWER EACH PERSON."

I will invest my time and energy into loving my body as it is. I may want to change certain things about my body, but I still love and accept it in its current state. My desire to change stems from my desire to be the best version of myself. I love myself at every size. I know I deserve to feel energized, full of vitality, and excited about my body and appearance. I will make the changes to achieve that feeling, starting today.

MARCH 15

I am constantly evolving to become the best version of myself.

PSALM 19:14 (KJV)

"LET THE WORDS OF MY MOUTH AND THE MEDITATION OF MY HEART BE ACCEPTABLE IN YOUR SIGHT, O LORD, MY ROCK AND MY REDEEMER."

Striving to be at my best is a direct reflection of my faith in God. When I work to be at my best, I am showing God that I love Him, and I want to bring Him glory in all that I do. I am dedicated to evolving, and that shows in my thoughts, words, and actions. I will continue working on myself, loving myself, and loving others. God sees my efforts, and He is proud of me. I take time to celebrate my progress today.

I speak to myself as someone I love dearly. My inner voice directly impacts my mental health and emotional wellbeing.

ISAIAH 55:11 (NIV)

"SO SHALL MY WORD BE THAT GOES OUT FROM MY MOUTH; IT SHALL NOT RETURN TO ME EMPTY, BUT IT SHALL ACCOMPLISH THAT WHICH I PURPOSE, AND SHALL SUCCEED IN THE THING FOR WHICH I SENT IT."

I love myself. I accept myself as I am. I treat myself with love and care every day. In doing this, I teach others to do the same. I am mindful about the words I say and the thoughts I think. I nurture my creativity and spirituality with things that bring me joy.

I am special. I am important. I am loved. I am enough.

I am in tune with my body's needs.

PROVERBS 18:20 (ESV)

"FROM THE FRUIT OF A MAN'S MOUTH HIS STOMACH IS SATISFIED; HE IS SATISFIED BY THE YIELD OF HIS LIPS."

Focusing on my body's needs is not just about physical health but also a deep acknowledgment that my body is a temple of the Holy Spirit. By actively listening to what my body requires—whether it's rest, nourishment, hydration, or movement—I honor God's design for wellbeing.

I remind myself daily that self-care is not selfish; it's a vital part of our spiritual and physical stewardship. In this harmonious connection with my body, I find balance, resilience, and strength.

Prioritizing my connection with my body is a sacred act of worship and self-love, grounded in faith and gratitude.

I set clear boundaries and protect my mental health by honoring those boundaries.

1 PETER 5:7 (NKJV)

"CASTING ALL YOUR CARE UPON HIM; FOR HE CARES FOR YOU."

My wellbeing, both physical and spiritual, is a divine gift. By establishing boundaries, I create a space for inner peace and spiritual growth, allowing me to serve others from a place of abundance and strength. This is my daily reminder that my mental health is precious and worth safeguarding. What are three ways I can set boundaries today?

I am deserving of happiness and fulfillment; I pursue it with my daily thoughts, words, and actions.

JOHN 15:11 (ESV)

"THESE THINGS I HAVE SPOKEN TO YOU, SO THAT MY JOY MAY BE IN YOU, AND THAT YOUR JOY MAY BE MADE FULL."

God's love and purpose for me extends far beyond my self-doubt or limitation. By consciously choosing positivity, gratitude, and faith each day, I can align my life with His abundant grace.

Joy and fulfillment are not fleeting moments but enduring gifts from God, meant to be experienced in every aspect of life. In pursuing them with intention, I honor His plan and inspire others to do the same.

I am deserving of the happiness and fulfillment that God offers, and by choosing to pursue it daily, I become a living testament to His love, grace, and boundless blessings.

I am available to journal about my feelings and experiences.

HABAKKUK 2:2 (KJV)

"THEN THE LORD ANSWERED ME AND SAID: 'WRITE THE VISION AND MAKE *IT* PLAIN ON TABLETS, THAT HE MAY RUN WHO READS IT.'"

Journaling is more than just putting pen to paper; it's a sacred practice of self-reflection and emotional release. By being available to journal, I create a safe space to explore my thoughts, feelings, and inner struggles. It's in these moments of vulnerability that I will find clarity, healing, and a deeper connection with God.

Through journaling, I allow my emotions to flow freely, releasing the burdens that weigh on my heart and mind. This practice not only nurtures my mental and emotional wellbeing but also strengthens my faith, as I can see His guidance and grace reflected in my words. I embrace the transformative power of journaling, recognizing it as a valuable tool for self-discovery and a means to foster a closer relationship with God through the authentic expression of my emotions.

I release the need for approval from others; validation is for parking, not people.

HEBREWS 10: 35-36 (NIV)

"SO DO NOT THROW AWAY YOUR CONFIDENCE; IT WILL BE RICHLY REWARDED.

You need to persevere so that when you have done the will of God, you will receive what he has promised."

Seeking validation from others can be a never-ending quest that leaves me feeling empty and unfulfilled. The true path to inner peace and self-worth lies in validating myself through faith and self-acceptance.

God's love is my ultimate validation! I anchor my self-worth in His unwavering grace, and I find an unshakeable foundation for confidence and authenticity. By recognizing my inherent value as His beloved daughter, I will free myself from the need for external approval.

I turn inward, embrace my unique qualities, and acknowledge my worthiness as a reflection of God's perfect design. When I validate myself from within, I will not only find lasting fulfillment but also inspire others to do the same, ultimately fostering a community of self-assured individuals rooted in faith and self-love.

I teach people how to treat me by showing myself love, grace, and acceptance.

JOHN 1:16 (NIV)

"OUT OF HIS FULLNESS WE HAVE ALL RECEIVED GRACE IN PLACE OF GRACE ALREADY GIVEN."

The way I treat myself sets the standard for how others treat me. By demonstrating a genuine love for myself and extending grace and acceptance to my imperfections, I invite others to do the same. This affirmation underscores the transforming power of self-respect and self-compassion, reminding me and those I inspire that we are worthy of kindness and understanding from ourselves and from others. By leading with self-love, I cultivate healthier relationships and empower those around me to embrace the same principles, creating a positive ripple effect of love and acceptance that can change lives and communities for the better.

I celebrate my strengths and use them to improve all areas of my life.

JAMES 1:2-4 (ESV)

"COUNT IT ALL JOY, MY BROTHERS, WHEN YOU MEET TRIALS OF VARIOUS KINDS, FOR YOU KNOW THAT THE TESTING OF YOUR FAITH PRODUCES STEADFASTNESS. AND LET STEADFASTNESS HAVE ITS FULL EFFECT, THAT YOU MAY BE PERFECT AND COMPLETE, LACKING IN NOTHING."

God has gifted each of me with unique talents and abilities, and it is my responsibility to recognize and honor them. By celebrating my strengths, I not only boost my self-confidence but also unlock the potential for growth and impact. Whether it's in the realm of health, fitness, or wellness, acknowledging my strengths empowers me to set ambitious goals, overcome challenges, and inspire others with my journey.

I am a vessel of God's grace and purpose, and when I leverage my strengths to improve my life, I am fulfilling His divine plan and becoming a beacon of inspiration for others on their own path to self-discovery and personal growth.

I embrace stillness and inner peace. In silencing the noise, I can hear God's voice speaking through my intuition.

PSALM 46:10 (NIV)

"HE SAYS, 'BE STILL, AND KNOW THAT I AM GOD; I WILL BE EXALTED AMONG THE NATIONS, I WILL BE EXALTED IN THE EARTH.'"

In the midst of life's constant hustle and bustle, it's in the quiet moments that I can truly hear God's voice speaking through my intuition. By silencing the noise of the world, I create a sacred space for His guidance and wisdom to resonate within me. It's in this inner peace that I find clarity, purpose, and the strength to navigate life's challenges. I have a direct line to the divine within me, and by nurturing stillness and inner peace, I can tap into the spring of God's grace, allowing His voice to guide me on my journey toward health, fitness, and wellness, as well as every other facet of my life.

I do not punish myself for making mistakes. I recognize that I am human and that making mistakes is how I learn.

PROVERBS 24:16 (ESV)

"FOR THE RIGHTEOUS FALLS SEVEN TIMES AND RISES AGAIN, BUT THE WICKED STUMBLE IN TIMES OF CALAMITY."

I embrace the understanding that I am human and that making mistakes is an essential part of the learning process. My journey toward health, fitness, and wellness is not linear, and it's in the moments of stumbling that I find the greatest opportunities for growth.

By extending grace to myself, I create an environment of self-compassion and resilience. t My worth is not defined by my mistakes but by my willingness to learn and grow from them. Through faith and self-acceptance, I navigate life's challenges with a sense of grace and confidence, ultimately becoming stronger, wiser, and more resilient.

I create space for myself and all my feelings and emotions without being controlled by them.

PROVERBS 16:32 (ESV)

"WHOEVER IS SLOW TO ANGER IS BETTER THAN THE MIGHTY, AND HE WHO RULES HIS SPIRIT THAN HE WHO TAKES A CITY."

My emotions are a natural and essential part of my human experience, and by acknowledging and embracing them, I empower myself to navigate life with authenticity and resilience. It's in this space of self-acceptance that I find strength and clarity, enabling myself to respond to challenges with grace and faith.

I am not defined by my emotions but rather by my ability to choose my responses and lean on my faith as an unwavering source of guidance and support. In doing so, I will become more balanced, whole, and resilient on my journey to health, fitness, and overall wellness.

I stop negative thoughts dead in their tracks and replace them with ten positive thoughts.

PSALM 1:2 (ESV)

"BUT HIS DELIGHT IS IN THE LAW OF THE LORD, AND IN HIS LAW HE MEDITATES DAY AND NIGHT."

I cultivate a mindset of positivity and faith. By redirecting my thoughts toward gratitude, hope, and love, I transform my outlook and strengthen my connection with God.

I have the power to shape my thoughts and, in turn, shape my life. I embrace the transformative potential of a positive mindset and watch my world change!

I release old patterns and thoughts that do not promote my healthy lifestyle.

ROMANS 12:2 (NIV)

"DO NOT CONFORM TO THE PATTERN OF THIS WORLD BUT BE TRANSFORMED BY THE RENEWING OF YOUR MIND. THEN YOU WILL BE ABLE TO TEST AND APPROVE WHAT GOD'S WILL IS—HIS GOOD, PLEASING AND PERFECT WILL."

I have the capacity for transformation and growth, and it begins by releasing the weight of the past that holds me back. Freeing myself from negative patterns and thoughts creates space for positive change and progress on my journey toward health, fitness, and wellness.

I am defined by my ability to choose a brighter and healthier future. Through faith and determination, I break free from the chains of old habits and embrace the empowering potential of a renewed mindset, propelling me toward my best self and God's intended plan for my wellbeing.

Resting restores my body and mind. I invest time in rest as I know it allows me to be at my best.

PSALM 4:8 (NIV)

"IN PEACE I WILL LIE DOWN AND SLEEP, FOR YOU ALONE LORD, MAKE ME DWELL IN SAFETY."

Rest is not a sign of weakness but rather a source of strength and rejuvenation. It's in these moments of stillness and renewal that I allow my body to heal, my mind to reset, and my spirit to find peace. By investing time in rest, I honor the divine design of my body and prepare myself to be at my absolute best.

Self-care and rest are essential components of a holistic and vibrant life. Through faith, I understand that rest is a gift from God, and by embracing it, I equip myself to face life's challenges with resilience, clarity, and an unwavering commitment to my wellbeing.

I honor and embrace my uniqueness with love. I accept all my flaws, quirks, and shortcomings.

ROMANS 5:8 (ESV)

"BUT GOD SHOWS HIS LOVE FOR US IN THAT WHILE WE WERE STILL SINNERS, CHRIST DIED FOR US."

God created each of us, including me, as wonderfully unique individuals with our own set of flaws, quirks, and shortcomings. It is through accepting and loving myself just as I am that I find true authenticity and inner peace.

My perceived imperfections are simply part of my divine design. By embracing my uniqueness with love and gratitude, I become a vessel of His grace, radiating light and inspiring others to do the same. In accepting myself fully, I discover the freedom to pursue a holistic wellbeing from a place of self-love and self-acceptance.

I operate at my best every day because I take excellent care of myself - mind, body, and soul.

EPHESIANS 5:29 (NIV)

"AFTER ALL, NO ONE EVER HATED THEIR OWN BODY, BUT THEY FEED AND CARE FOR THEIR BODY, JUST AS CHRIST DOES THE CHURCH."

I understand that self-care is a necessary act of stewardship. I nurture my mind with positive thoughts, my body with nourishing choices, and my soul with faith and reflection. I create a harmonious balance that empowers me to thrive in every aspect of life, including health, fitness, and overall wellness. My self-care journey is a testament to God's grace, guiding me to be my best self for His glory and the betterment of others.

Let your Life be affirmed

April:

Embracing Change and Cultivating Healthy Friendships

Being Flexible and Adaptable Throughout the Seasons of Life

One of the most important lessons I have learned on my journey is that the only constant is change. Change can sometimes feel debilitating and frightening because it can bring about uncertainty. However, that same uncertainty can fuel you to keep going if you let it. It helps if you have the right people around you.

This month, let's delve into the profound significance of these qualities in our lives as believers and individuals seeking to lead purposeful, renewed lives. Each affirmation is centered around helping you to embrace change and the growth and transformation that happens when we open our minds and hearts to the new thing God is doing within us. This includes doing an "inventory check" of the friends in our circle.

I celebrate you, and I love you. I can't wait to see the awesome ways God moves in your life this month.

I am not resistant to change, for it is simply God's plan unfolding in my life.

2 CORINTHIANS 5:17 (ESV)

"THEREFORE, IF ANYONE IS IN CHRIST, HE IS A NEW CREATION. THE OLD HAS PASSED AWAY; BEHOLD, THE NEW HAS COME."

I wholeheartedly embrace change, recognizing it as a divine part of God's plan unfolding in my life. I approach every new opportunity, challenge, and endeavor with a beginner's mindset, eager to learn, adapt, and grow.

Life is a journey of continuous learning, and I am a lifelong student open to the wisdom and lessons that each experience brings. With God as my guide, I step boldly into the unknown, trusting that change is a pathway to personal and professional transformation.

In affirming these things, I not only navigate change with grace, but I also inspire others to do the same, fostering a community of resilient, adaptable, and lifelong learners who find purpose and fulfillment in embracing the ever-evolving chapters of life.

I spend time in nature, allowing God to speak to my soul.

JOB 12:7-10 (NIV)

"BUT ASK THE ANIMALS, AND THEY WILL TEACH YOU, OR THE BIRDS IN THE SKY, AND THEY WILL TELL YOU; OR SPEAK TO THE EARTH, AND IT WILL TEACH YOU, OR LET THE FISH IN THE SEA INFORM YOU. WHICH OF ALL THESE DOES NOT KNOW THAT THE HAND OF THE LORD HAS DONE THIS? IN HIS HAND IS THE LIFE OF EVERY CREATURE AND THE BREATH OF ALL MANKIND."

I cherish the profound human and divine connection to nature, recognizing it as a sacred space where I can quiet my mind and open my heart to the whispers of God. In the serene beauty of the natural world, I find solace, inspiration, and a profound sense of wonder. It's here that I feel the closest to the Creator as if the very essence of God infuses every tree, every river, and every breeze.

By spending time in nature, I allow God to speak to my soul, offering guidance, comfort, and a deep sense of belonging. This connection reminds me of the intricate tapestry of life and my role as a steward of His creation. It is in this divine union with nature that I find strength, purpose, and a rekindled spirit to help others discover the same profound connection, unlocking the transformative power of communion with the natural world.

I honor the beauty of the changing seasons of my life.

ECCLESIASTES 3:1 (NIV)

"THERE IS A TIME FOR EVERYTHING, AND A SEASON FOR EVERY ACTIVITY UNDER THE HEAVENS:"

Just as the seasons change, my life is also marked by moments of change, growth, and transition, all of which are ultimately for my greatest good. I know that these shifts, though at times challenging, are essential for my personal and professional evolution. By honoring the beauty of the changing seasons in life, I embrace the wisdom of God's plan unfolding.

It's in these transitions that I discover resilience, uncover new opportunities, and find the strength to adapt and thrive. I accept God's guidance in recognizing the transforming energy within change. I know that God is helping me to navigate life's seasons with grace, purpose, and unwavering faith. In doing so, I am unlocking my true potential and aligning self with the divine flow of life, where growth and blessings await at every turn.

I let go of what no longer serves me. I understand that things change for a reason, and I flow with the tides of my life.

2 CORINTHIANS 5:17 (ESV)

"THEREFORE, IF ANYONE IS IN CHRIST, HE IS A NEW CREATION. THE OLD HAS PASSED AWAY; BEHOLD, THE NEW HAS COME."

I understand the importance of identifying people and things that no longer serve me and gracefully letting them go. Life is a dynamic journey, and as I evolve, my needs and aspirations change. By releasing what no longer aligns with my growth and purpose, I make space for new opportunities and relationships that elevate my life.

Just as the tides ebb and flow, I understand that change is a natural part of my path. I embrace it with an open heart, knowing that things change for a reason and that each shift brings me closer to my true self. I navigate the currents of my life with courage and self-awareness. I embrace change as a catalyst for personal and professional transformation, recognizing that by letting go, room is created for the blessings that await me on the horizon.

I value my worth and refuse to compromise my self-respect for others' approval.

GALATIANS 1:10 (BSB)

"FOR AM I NOW SEEKING THE FAVOR OF MEN, OR OF GOD? OR AM I STRIVING TO PLEASE MEN? IF I WERE STILL TRYING TO PLEASE MEN, I WOULD NOT BE A BOND-SERVANT OF CHRIST."

I understand that knowing my worth and maintaining high self-esteem are foundational principles for my personal and professional success. I know the importance of valuing myself and refusing to compromise my self-respect for the approval of others.

I recognize my inherent worth, and therefore, I become steadfast in my authenticity and self-confidence. By doing so, I will lead a more fulfilling life and move closer to becoming the best version of myself.

I am worthy of genuine love and friendship without having to sacrifice my boundaries.

PROVERBS 18:24 (ESV)

"A MAN OF MANY COMPANIONS MAY COME TO RUIN, BUT THERE IS A FRIEND WHO STICKS CLOSER THAN A BROTHER."

Genuine friendship is a precious gift, especially when those friends are like-minded and in alignment with my direction in life. I understand the importance of nurturing relationships that uplift and support my spiritual and personal journey.

It's vital to honor my boundaries and recognize that I am worthy of authentic love and friendship without sacrificing my values or principles. True friends will respect my boundaries and walk alongside me in faith, sharing the joys and challenges of my journey. These relationships, rooted in mutual respect and shared purpose, will strengthen my resolve and provide a sense of belonging that enriches my life.

I attract healthy relationships by staying true to myself and setting clear boundaries.

1 CORINTHIANS 15:33 (ESV)

"DO NOT BE DECEIVED: "BAD COMPANY RUINS GOOD MORALS."

Attracting healthy relationships begins with staying true to my most authentic self and setting clear boundaries. I know the importance of authenticity and self-respect in cultivating meaningful connections. When I honor my true self and establish clear boundaries, I create a foundation of trust and mutual understanding.

I know that healthy relationships are built on respect, transparency, and shared values, and by staying true to who I am and what I stand for, I will naturally draw individuals who align with my purpose and vision.

In this way, I not only foster harmonious connections but also inspire others to embrace their authenticity and set healthy boundaries in their own lives. By surrounding myself with like-minded individuals who respect my boundaries, I create a supportive and uplifting community that empowers me to thrive in faith and purpose.

I prioritize my wellbeing and won't allow anyone to take advantage of my kindness.

PROVERBS 22:24-25 (NLT)

"DON'T BEFRIEND ANGRY PEOPLE OR ASSOCIATE WITH HOT-TEMPERED PEOPLE, OR YOU WILL LEARN TO BE LIKE THEM AND ENDANGER YOUR SOUL."

My kindness should never equate to vulnerability or allowing others to take advantage of me. By firmly prioritizing my own wellbeing and setting boundaries, I protect myself and exemplify the importance of self-respect and self-care.

I am a child of God, deserving of love and respect. In honoring my wellbeing and firmly guarding against those who may seek to exploit my kindness, I create a space of empowerment, self-love, and faith. From that place, I thrive and make a positive impact on those around me.

I express gratitude for the positive changes I see in myself and the people I love.

2 PETER 3:9 (NIV)

"THE LORD IS NOT SLOW IN KEEPING HIS PROMISE, AS SOME UNDERSTAND SLOWNESS. INSTEAD, HE IS PATIENT WITH YOU, NOT WANTING ANYONE TO PERISH, BUT EVERYONE TO COME TO REPENTANCE."

Gratitude is at the core of my Christian faith, and I am deeply thankful for the positive changes in my life. I recognize that every transformation, every step forward, is a testament to God's grace and guidance. By expressing gratitude for these changes, I acknowledge His hand in my journey and open myself to even greater blessings.

Each positive change serves as a reminder of God's love and faithfulness. I cultivate a personal culture of gratitude for the progress I have made and the blessings I have received. I know that this is just the beginning of more positive changes to come. I honor the indescribable power of God's presence and I invite His continued favor and grace into my life and the lives of the people I love.

I intentionally nourish authentic connections that are built on mutual respect and understanding.

ROMANS 1:12 (ESV)

"THAT IS, THAT WE MAY BE MUTUALLY ENCOURAGED BY EACH OTHER'S FAITH, BOTH YOURS AND MINE."

Cultivating positive relationships is a cornerstone of my Christian faith, and I intentionally invest my energy into helping them grow. Authentic connections built on mutual respect and understanding are invaluable, as they reflect God's love and grace in my life. By nourishing these relationships, I honor the divine within each individual and create a community of trust and support.

I recognize that the energy I invest in building and maintaining positive relationships not only enriches my life but also ripples out to touch the lives of others, spreading love, unity, and God's grace in our journey toward personal and professional fulfillment.

I trust my instincts to steer me toward my long-term collaborators and away from negative influences.

MATTHEW 10:16 (KJV)

"BEHOLD, I SEND YOU FORTH AS SHEEP IN THE MIDST OF WOLVES: BE YE THEREFORE WISE AS SERPENTS, AND HARMLESS AS DOVES."

I know that selecting the right friends is a significant aspect of my Christian journey. My circle of friends has the power to shape my life. I seek out friends who are positive influences - individuals who uplift and encourage me to make good decisions and engage in activities that contribute to my overall growth and development.

Trusting my instincts and divine guidance, I navigate toward those who align with my values and long-term aspirations. I actively create a supportive circle of friends who not only enrich my life but also inspire me to walk in faith, make wise choices, and continually evolve in the path of God's purpose. These relationships are a testament to the transformative significance of positive influences, nurturing my spiritual being and my personal development as I journey with others in faith and unity.

I am strong enough to make good choices, even in difficult situations.

PROVERBS 11:3 (NIV)

"THE INTEGRITY OF THE UPRIGHT GUIDES THEM, BUT THE UNFAITHFUL ARE DESTROYED BY THEIR DUPLICITY."

I resist temptation, and I consistently make the right choices, especially when no one is watching. This is a testament to my integrity and strength of character. I strive to demonstrate unwavering integrity and the inner strength to make virtuous choices in all circumstances.

I honor my commitment to God's principles and am known amongst my friends, family, and community as someone who walks with integrity. When I choose righteousness over temptation, I am demonstrating powerful affirmations of my faith and commitment to living a life that reflects God's grace and wisdom.

My self-worth is not determined by others' opinions, and I stand firm in my convictions.

JAMES 1:6 (ESV)

"BUT LET HIM ASK IN FAITH, WITH NO DOUBTING, FOR THE ONE WHO DOUBTS IS LIKE A WAVE OF THE SEA THAT IS DRIVEN AND TOSSED BY THE WIND."

Being strong-minded in my commitment to aligning my actions with my personal values is a crucial component of my Christian faith. I don't allow myself to be swayed by the behaviors or opinions of others. My self-worth is firmly rooted in God's love and purpose for my life. I stand resolute in my convictions, understanding that true strength comes from living in alignment with His principles.

While I value the perspectives of others, I do not let their opinions define my worth or the path I choose to follow. My faith in my beliefs empowers me to live authentically and lead by example, encouraging others to do the same and ultimately glorifying God in all that I do.

I live to please God, not people.

ROMANS 14:12 (ESV)

"SO THEN EACH OF US WILL GIVE AN ACCOUNT OF HIMSELF TO GOD."

Ceasing to be a people pleaser is an important step in honoring myself and living in alignment with my Christian faith. While it's natural to want to bring joy to others, I recognize the significance of prioritizing God's will and my own wellbeing and authenticity. Releasing people-pleasing thoughts and behaviors allows me to set healthy boundaries, maintain my self-respect, and stay true to my values.

It's through this self-honoring mindset that I can truly serve others from a place of love, authenticity, and faith. By letting go of the need for external validation, I find the freedom to embrace my purpose and encourage those I coach to do the same, fostering a community of empowered individuals who live authentically and radiate God's love in their endeavors.

I create space for relationships that uplift and support me. I release relationships that drain and distract me.

PROVERBS 13:20 (ESV)

"WHOEVER WALKS WITH THE WISE BECOMES WISE, BUT THE COMPANION OF FOOLS WILL SUFFER HARM."

Positive and healthy relationships are paramount in my life. I intentionally create space for connections that uplift and support me on my journey. These relationships are like nourishing soil, allowing me to grow and thrive in faith and purpose. I also recognize the importance of releasing relationships that drain my energy and distract me from my path. Letting go of such connections is an act of self-care and self-respect, allowing me to prioritize my wellbeing and stay focused on God's plan for my life.

I fill my cup first, allowing me to give from my overflow, not my deficit.

PSALM 23:5 (ESV)

"YOU PREPARE A TABLE BEFORE ME IN THE PRESENCE OF MY ENEMIES. YOU ANOINT MY HEAD WITH OIL; MY CUP OVERFLOWS."

I will no longer run on fumes throughout my day. I will no longer rush from this meeting to that appointment to the next event—barely taking a moment for myself. It is so easy to do, and yet it is not optimal to living my best life. I cannot pour from an empty cup. So, I fill my cup first. I make sure that I am at the top of my priority list and await radical improvement in all areas of my life.

I pray for the health and wellbeing of my friends.

LUKE 6:31 (ESV)

"AND AS YOU WISH THAT OTHERS WOULD DO TO YOU, DO SO TO THEM."

Praying for the health and wellbeing of my friends is not just a practice but a deep expression of love and faith. I believe in the power of prayer to bring comfort, healing, and strength to those I hold dear. I lift their names in prayer, trusting that God's grace and love will surround them in their times of need.

By interceding on their behalf, I strengthen the bonds of our friendship while manifesting God's blessings in their lives. In praying for my friends, I cherish the beauty of community and the importance of supporting one another on our personal and spiritual journeys. I know that my faith-filled prayers have the power to bring about positive change and a sense of peace that can only come from Him.

I speak words of life and positivity to and about my friends.

JOHN 15:12-15 (ESV)

"THIS IS MY COMMANDMENT, THAT YOU LOVE ONE ANOTHER AS I HAVE LOVED YOU. GREATER LOVE HAS NO ONE THAN THIS, THAT SOMEONE LAY DOWN HIS LIFE FOR HIS FRIENDS. YOU ARE MY FRIENDS IF YOU DO WHAT I COMMAND YOU. NO LONGER DO I CALL YOU SERVANTS, FOR THE SERVANT DOES NOT KNOW WHAT HIS MASTER IS DOING; BUT I HAVE CALLED YOU FRIENDS, FOR ALL THAT I HAVE HEARD FROM MY FATHER I HAVE MADE KNOWN TO YOU."

I acknowledge the power of speaking words of life and positivity to and about my friends. I understand that my words carry immense weight and influence. By speaking words of encouragement, affirmation, and love to my friends, I uplift their spirits and create an environment of trust and support.

My words have the power to inspire, heal, and strengthen my connections, aligning with God's message of love and compassion. Through my positive words, I become a vessel of His grace, radiating His light in my relationships and fostering a community of empowered and uplifted individuals who are better equipped to face life's challenges with faith and resilience.

I take personal inventory of the relationships in my life, adding and subtracting accordingly.

PROVERBS 20:6 (ESV)

"MANY A MAN PROCLAIMS HIS OWN STEADFAST LOVE, BUT A FAITHFUL MAN WHO CAN FIND?"

Taking a personal inventory of the relationships in my life is a vital practice on my journey. I am mindful of ensuring that I have the right people around me—individuals who align with my values, purpose, and faith. Just as in business, where I assess my assets and liabilities, I recognize the importance of periodically evaluating the people who impact my life. This includes adding those who inspire, support, and uplift me while subtracting those whose influence may not align with God's plan for my wellbeing.

This sacred practice allows me to create a circle of authentic and nurturing relationships that enhance my growth and spiritual journey. It is through this intentional curation of connections that I not only honor myself but also encourage others to do the same, fostering a community that radiates God's love and purpose in all that we do.

I prioritize God's Word, my peace, and my purpose, keeping them at the forefront of my mind each day and allowing them to govern my actions.

2 THESSALONIANS 3:16 (NIV)

"NOW MAY THE LORD OF PEACE HIMSELF GIVE YOU PEACE AT ALL TIMES IN EVERY WAY. THE LORD BE WITH ALL OF YOU."

Focusing on my inner peace and God's purpose for my life is paramount for me. I prioritize God's Word, my peace, and my purpose, holding them at the forefront of my mind each day. These guiding principles govern my actions and decisions, ensuring that I am aligned with His divine plan. By keeping faith as my compass, I navigate life's challenges and successes with grace and unwavering conviction. This commitment not only allows me to fulfill God's purpose but also inspires those I engage with to embark on their own journeys of faith, inner peace, and purposeful living, creating a continuing flow of positive transformation and spiritual growth.

I have plans of my own, but I remain open and flexible to God's timing.

ISAIAH 43:19 (NIV)

"SEE, I AM DOING A NEW THING! NOW IT SPRINGS UP; DO YOU NOT PERCEIVE IT? I AM MAKING A WAY IN THE WILDERNESS AND STREAMS IN THE WASTELAND."

Remaining open and flexible to God's timing is a cornerstone of my approach as a Christian. While I may have my own plans and aspirations, I recognize that His divine timing surpasses my own understanding. By embracing this mindset, I am prepared to adapt and flow with the currents of His purpose, even when it deviates from my own timeline. It is in these moments of surrender and trust that I discover the true beauty of His plan unfolding. This openness to change not only enhances my journey but also serves as an example to those I love, inspiring them to navigate life's twists and turns with faith, resilience, and unwavering trust in God's perfect timing.

My peace is priceless and non-negotiable, and I do not entertain people, places, or things that disturb it.

1 PETER 3:11 (NIV)

"THEY MUST TURN FROM EVIL AND DO GOOD; THEY MUST SEEK PEACE AND PURSUE IT."

Protecting my peace at all costs is non-negotiable for me. I recognize that peace is a priceless gift from God, and I cannot allow anyone or anything to disturb it. If a situation or relationship threatens my peace, I understand that the cost is simply too high, and I cannot afford to compromise my inner serenity.

My commitment to guarding my peace is an act of self-respect and faith, ensuring that I remain aligned with God's purpose and maintain a spirit of tranquility and resilience in all that I do.

I hold space for my friends; they know they can come to me for love and support.

PROVERBS 18:24 (NIV)

"ONE WHO HAS UNRELIABLE FRIENDS SOON COMES TO RUIN, BUT THERE IS A FRIEND WHO STICKS CLOSER THAN A BROTHER."

Being there for my friends is not just a choice; it's a calling deeply rooted in my faith as a believer. I hold a sacred space for my friends, creating an environment where they know they can turn to me for love, support, and understanding. In return, they do the same for me, uplifting me when I am down and celebrating with me when I am happy. This beautiful reciprocity is an earthly example of God's love for us.

Just as God showers His grace upon me, I aim to extend His love and compassion to those I hold dear. Whether in times of joy or challenges, I stand as a steady pillar of support, fostering a community of trust and mutual care. This commitment to being there for my friends reflects the essence of Christian fellowship, where we uplift one another in faith and love, ultimately strengthening our bonds and bringing glory to God through our compassionate and supportive actions.

I know I cannot bring old patterns and mindsets into a new season; I will grow, evolve, and flow with God.

JEREMIAH 29:11 (NIV)

"FOR I KNOW THE PLANS I HAVE FOR YOU," DECLARES THE LORD, "PLANS TO PROSPER YOU AND NOT TO HARM YOU, PLANS TO GIVE YOU HOPE AND A FUTURE."

I know that embracing change and adapting to new seasons is a vital aspect of my Christian journey. I recognize that I cannot bring old patterns and mindsets into a new season of growth and purpose. I commit to growing, evolving, and flowing with God's divine plan.

Just as nature undergoes transformation each season, I know that I, too, need to renew or shed old habits and ways of thinking to align with God's purpose. My openness to change allows me to thrive in faith and resilience, navigating life's transitions with grace and trust in His guidance.

I use my God-given gifts and abilities to create the life that I want.

ECCLESIASTES 5:18-20 (KJV)

"HERE IS WHAT I HAVE SEEN: *IT IS* GOOD AND FITTING *FOR ONE* TO EAT AND DRINK, AND TO ENJOY THE GOOD OF ALL HIS LABOR IN WHICH HE TOILS UNDER THE SUN ALL THE DAYS OF HIS LIFE WHICH GOD GIVES HIM; FOR IT *IS* HIS HERITAGE."

Indeed, God has bestowed upon me a remarkable power when He created me in His image. He made me in His likeness, granting me the ability to create, design, and shape my life according to His divine plan.

This reminds me that I am never powerless, but in fact, I am deeply powerful beyond measure. I wholeheartedly embrace the gifts and abilities He has given me, using them to co-create a life that aligns with His purpose and grace. I honor His divine design, and I walk in my limitless potential to manifest His blessings in my life.

I encourage my friends to pursue their dreams and support them in doing so.

MATTHEW 18:20 (NIV)

"FOR WHERE TWO OR THREE ARE GATHERED IN MY NAME, THERE AM I AMONG THEM."

Encouraging my friends is a beautiful and fulfilling part of my journey. I look forward to finding ways to uplift my friends. I find ways to motivate them to pursue their dreams. I am their number one cheerleader. As I walk alongside them in faith and purpose, I find immense joy in witnessing their growth and accomplishments, and I love celebrating their wins with them.

My voice is one of understanding, upliftment, and inspiration, reminding them that they can achieve greatness with God's guidance. My friends know they can always look to me for words of affirmation, validation, and encouragement. By fostering an environment of encouragement and belief in one another's potential, we create a community that thrives in love, unity, and the shared pursuit of God-given aspirations.

I am not threatened or intimidated by my friends' success because I know there is enough to go around.

2 CORINTHIANS 9:8 (NIV)

"AND GOD IS ABLE TO BLESS YOU ABUNDANTLY, SO THAT IN ALL THINGS AT ALL TIMES, HAVING ALL THAT YOU NEED, YOU WILL ABOUND IN EVERY GOOD WORK."

Avoiding jealousy and envy amongst my friends is a testament to the strength of my relationships and the depth of my faith. I stand firm in the belief that there is an abundance of blessings and success to go around, and I celebrate my friends' achievements with wholehearted joy. I know that they celebrate my accomplishments with the same excitement and joy. We are proud of each other, and we know that when one of us wins, we all win.

In God's infinite grace, there is no room for comparison or competition. Comparison is the thief of joy. It also causes me to view things through a distorted lens because we are all unique and on our individual paths. We experience different things at different times and seasons throughout our lives.

I understand that my friends' achievements do not diminish my own potential or blessings. Instead, they inspire me to reach higher, grow stronger, and walk in faith, knowing that as we encourage each other's journeys, we collectively glorify God in all that we do.

I invest time, energy, and resources in things and people that will help me grow.

DEUTERONOMY 28:12 (NIV)

"THE LORD WILL OPEN THE HEAVENS, THE STOREHOUSE OF HIS BOUNTY, TO SEND RAIN ON YOUR LAND IN SEASON AND TO BLESS ALL THE WORK OF YOUR HANDS. YOU WILL LEND TO MANY NATIONS BUT WILL BORROW FROM NONE."

Life is a precious gift, and I am committed to making the most of it by nurturing relationships and pursuits that inspire and challenge me to become the best version of myself. I understand that true growth requires intentional investment, and I am determined to sow seeds that will yield a harvest of wisdom, love, and resilience.

In this journey of faith and personal development, I am guided by the understanding that by investing wisely, I honor God's plan and also inspire my friends to do the same. Together, we cultivate a community of individuals who thrive in purpose and unity.

I consistently perform random acts of kindness for my friends. I love finding ways to surprise and delight them.

ACTS 28:2 (NASB1995)

"THE NATIVES SHOWED US EXTRAORDINARY KINDNESS; FOR BECAUSE OF THE RAIN THAT HAD SET IN AND BECAUSE OF THE COLD, THEY KINDLED A FIRE AND RECEIVED US ALL."

Consistently performing random acts of kindness for my friends reflects the love and faith that guide my life's journey. Through these small gestures, I sow seeds of love and strengthen the bonds of friendship. Just as God's love is boundless and overflowing, I aim to overflow with kindness and compassion toward those I hold dear. With my random acts of kindness, I uplift spirits and inspire the reciprocity of generosity and love.

I am loyal to and thankful for the meaningful relationships I have cultivated.

PROVERBS 21:21 (NASB1995)

"ONE WHO PURSUES RIGHTEOUSNESS AND LOYALTY FINDS LIFE, RIGHTEOUSNESS, AND HONOR."

I am fiercely loyal to those who have stood by my side, knowing that the bonds we share reflect God's love and purpose in our lives. Gratitude fills my heart for the moments of joy, support, and growth that these relationships have brought me. I believe that by nurturing such meaningful connections, I honor God's plan and create a tapestry of love and unity that radiates His grace in our journey of faith and personal development.

Let your Life be affirmed

May:

Marriage, Parenting and Family Life

Understanding God's Purpose for You and The People You Love

Marriage and family are profound gifts from God, reflecting the divine plan and model described in God's Word. In scripture, we find the beautiful analogy of Christ's love for the church as His bride, a love that is sacrificial, unchanging, and unconditional. Couples are encouraged to model their relationships and family dynamics after this divine example, embracing the principles of love, grace, forgiveness, and unity.

Each day spent with our spouses and family members is a classroom of comprehensive life lessons. It's within the bonds of marriage and family that we learn the art of selflessness, patience, and compassion. We discover the power of forgiveness and the strength of unity.

In the sacred journey of marriage and family life, we witness the sanctity of life, the nurturing of faith, and the joy of growing together in God's grace. We are reminded of our roles as husbands and wives, parents and children, with responsibilities rooted in love and respect. By following the divine example set forth in the Bible, we create homes filled with love, faith, and purpose. We honor God's plan and reflect His love and grace in our most cherished relationships.

If you are single and desiring to be married, I encourage you to manifest the loving marriage and family that you desire, using these affirmations as a blueprint for how you want your future marriage to feel. God gave you the desire to be married and have a family, and His Word does not return to Him void. Trust that He is preparing you now, in your singleness, for the life that you desire.

I consider my spouse in decisions that will impact them.

GENESIS 2:24 (ESV)

"THEREFORE, A MAN SHALL LEAVE HIS FATHER AND HIS MOTHER AND HOLD FAST TO HIS WIFE, AND THEY SHALL BECOME ONE FLESH."

Consulting with my spouse in decision-making is a practice that reflects the love, respect, and unity that outlines our partnership. I understand the importance of considering my spouse in decisions that will impact them, for our paths are intertwined in God's divine plan.

We share not only our joys but also our responsibilities, finances, and personal space. By consistently practicing open communication and mutual consideration with my spouse, I am honoring my commitment to our union and our life together.

I show grace and love to my partner, especially when I don't think they deserve it.

COLOSSIANS 3:18-19 (NIV)

"WIVES, SUBMIT TO YOUR HUSBANDS, AS IS FITTING IN THE LORD. HUSBANDS, LOVE YOUR WIVES, AND DO NOT BE HARSH WITH THEM."

In the sacred union of marriage, showing grace is not only a choice but an embodiment of the boundless love and compassion that flows from God's heart. I understand the significance of extending grace and love to my partner, especially in moments when I may think they don't deserve it. Just as God's grace is freely given to us, so, too, do I strive to offer it to my spouse.

It's through these acts of unconditional love that I emulate the divine example set forth in the Bible, where forgiveness and grace are central themes. By showing grace, I nurture a loving and forgiving atmosphere within our marriage but also inspire a culture of understanding, growth, and support. In this journey of faith and partnership, grace becomes a cornerstone, allowing us to navigate life's challenges with humility, compassion, and the enduring love that mirrors God's grace for us.

I am committed to open and honest communication in my marriage.

EPHESIANS 4:25 (ESV)

"THEREFORE, HAVING PUT AWAY FALSEHOOD, LET EACH ONE OF YOU SPEAK THE TRUTH WITH HIS NEIGHBOR, FOR WE ARE MEMBERS ONE OF ANOTHER."

I affirm my commitment to open communication. I create a space where my partner and I can express our feelings, needs, and concerns without fear of judgment or rejection. It sets the foundation for understanding and resolving conflicts, as well as fostering a deeper emotional connection. Just as God invites us into a relationship with Him based on truth and transparency, I believe that my spouse and I should share our hearts openly, even when it's uncomfortable.

It's through candid conversations that we foster understanding, trust, and intimacy. I honor our commitment to one another by speaking truth with love and respect, resolving conflicts with grace, and celebrating our joys together. In this way, we not only strengthen our marital bond but also set an example for our family and community, reflecting God's call for authentic and heartfelt communication in all our relationships.

Parenting is my opportunity to practice showing God's unconditional love and grace to my children.

PROVERBS 22:6 (ESV)

"TRAIN UP A CHILD IN THE WAY HE SHOULD GO; EVEN WHEN HE IS OLD HE WILL NOT DEPART FROM IT."

As a parent, I embrace the beautiful responsibility of showing my children love and affection every day. I strive to mirror God's divine and unconditional love in my interactions with my little ones. Through hugs, kisses, kind words, and quality time, I create a nurturing environment where they can flourish and grow.

I understand that love is the foundation upon which our family is built, and it is through these daily expressions of love that we foster strong bonds, trust, and a deep sense of belonging. In this journey of parenthood, I am guided by the understanding that love is the greatest gift we can give to our children, and it is through this love that we reflect God's grace and compassion in our family's life.

I work together with my spouse, keeping in mind that my spouse is my teammate, not my opponent.

1 CORINTHIANS 13:4-7 (ESV)

"LOVE IS PATIENT AND KIND; LOVE DOES NOT ENVY OR BOAST; IT IS NOT ARROGANT OR RUDE. IT DOES NOT INSIST ON ITS OWN WAY; IT IS NOT IRRITABLE OR RESENTFUL; IT DOES NOT REJOICE AT WRONGDOING BUT REJOICES WITH THE TRUTH. LOVE BEARS ALL THINGS, BELIEVES ALL THINGS, HOPES ALL THINGS, ENDURES ALL THINGS."

In the beautiful dance of married life, I approach every challenge and endeavor, knowing that my spouse is not my opponent but my cherished teammate. We are partners in this journey, bound by love and a shared commitment to our family's wellbeing.

Together, we understand that our strengths complement each other, and our differences enrich our collective wisdom. We approach our challenges as opportunities for growth and collaboration, always supporting and uplifting one another.

In every aspect of our journey, we work together as a team, knowing that our love and faith are the cornerstones upon which we build a harmonious and thriving family life.

I focus on what my partner gets right, and I praise him/her for it with words of affirmation.

EPHESIANS 4:2 (ESV)

"WITH ALL HUMILITY AND GENTLENESS, WITH PATIENCE, BEARING WITH ONE ANOTHER IN LOVE."

In the sacred covenant of marriage, I choose to focus on what my partner gets right, and I make it a practice to praise them for it with words of affirmation. God showers us with His love and grace; I will shower my spouse with that same love and grace. I choose to see and celebrate the goodness in my spouse.

Through uplifting words and genuine appreciation, I strive to nurture an atmosphere of love, encouragement, and gratitude in our relationship. By recognizing and affirming their strengths and efforts, we create a bond that grows stronger with each passing day. It is through this act of praise and affirmation that we honor God's call to love and uplift one another, fostering a marriage filled with joy, unity, and enduring love.

I encourage my children to discover their gifts and talents.

DEUTERONOMY 6:7 (ESV)

"YOU SHALL TEACH THEM DILIGENTLY TO YOUR SONS AND SHALL TALK OF THEM WHEN YOU SIT IN YOUR HOUSE AND WHEN YOU WALK BY THE WAY AND WHEN YOU LIE DOWN AND WHEN YOU RISE UP."

As a parent, I am deeply committed to encouraging and motivating my children to discover their unique gifts and talents. God has created each of us with purpose and intention, and my children are blessed with their own set of extraordinary abilities.

God has entrusted me with the precious souls of my children. It is my responsibility and privilege to provide them with a loving and nurturing environment where they can explore, learn, and grow into the individuals God has designed them to be. Through words of encouragement, support, and belief in their potential, I inspire them to embrace their passions and talents with enthusiasm. In doing so, I empower them to walk confidently on their path, knowing that they are loved, valued, and capable of achieving greatness in God's eyes.

I encourage my partner to become the best version of themselves, and I find inspiring ways to help them do it.

PROVERBS 27:17 (NIV)

"AS IRON SHARPENS IRON, SO ONE PERSON SHARPENS ANOTHER."

I am committed to encouraging my partner to become the best version of themselves. It is a privilege to walk alongside them, providing support and inspiration as they navigate their path of growth and self-discovery.

I know that in a loving partnership, we lift each other higher, recognizing that our individual flourishing contributes to the strength of our union. I actively seek out ways to empower and motivate my spouse, knowing that their success and fulfillment reflect our shared commitment to love, encourage, and inspire one another. Together, we embark on a journey of self-improvement and growth, guided by God's grace and the boundless love we have for each other.

I prioritize spending quality time with my children giving them my undivided attention.

3 JOHN 1:4 (NASB1995)

"I HAVE NO GREATER JOY THAN THIS, TO HEAR OF MY CHILDREN WALKING IN THE TRUTH."

In the beautiful tapestry of family life, I prioritize spending quality time with my children, giving them the precious gift of my undivided attention. My children deserve my full presence and engagement. I understand that in these moments, I am creating lasting memories and fostering deep connections that will shape their lives. Whether it's reading a bedtime story, playing games, or simply having heart-to-heart conversations, I cherish these moments of togetherness.

By prioritizing quality time with my children, I am strengthening our family bonds while nurturing their sense of love, security, and belonging. I mirror God's love and grace in our family unit, creating a legacy of cherished moments and profound love.

I tell my children what they are good at and encourage them in areas where they need improvement and growth.

PROVERBS 13:24 (NASB1995)

"HE WHO WITHHOLDS HIS ROD HATES HIS SON, BUT HE WHO LOVES HIM DISCIPLINES HIM DILIGENTLY."

In the beautiful journey of parenthood, I make it a point to celebrate my children's strengths and talents but also to lovingly guide them in areas where they may need improvement and growth. I am careful to show them discipline with love.

Just as God has entrusted me with their care and nurturing, I take a balanced approach to disciplining them. I offer heartfelt praise and encouragement for their achievements, fostering their confidence and self-esteem. Simultaneously, I offer gentle guidance and support in areas where they face challenges, knowing that through patience and perseverance, they will blossom into the remarkable individuals God intended them to be. By recognizing both their gifts and areas for growth, I empower my children to embrace their full potential, guided by the love and grace that flows through our family unit.

I speak to my children lovingly, knowing that my words become their inner voice.

PROVERBS 16:24 (NIV)

"GRACIOUS WORDS ARE A HONEYCOMB, SWEET TO THE SOUL AND HEALING TO THE BONES."

In the sacred role of parenting, I speak to my children lovingly, fully aware that my words have the power to shape their inner voice and self-worth. With every word, I aim to uplift, motivate, and encourage them, nurturing their hearts and minds with the warmth of my love.

By speaking to them lovingly and with kindness, I offer them a safe and nurturing environment where they can flourish and grow into the beautiful souls God intended them to be. In this way, I not only mirror God's love in our family but also empower my children to carry that love within them as their guiding light.

I am a loving and nurturing mother, and I teach my children to be authentic in who they are.

ROMANS 9:8 (NASB1995)

"THAT IS, IT IS NOT THE CHILDREN OF THE FLESH WHO ARE CHILDREN OF GOD, BUT THE CHILDREN OF THE PROMISE ARE REGARDED AS DESCENDANTS."

I know that motherhood is sacred. I am steadfast in my commitment to being a loving and nurturing presence in my children's lives. I understand that one of the greatest gifts I can offer them is the encouragement to be authentic to who they are.

I strive to create a home where my children feel cherished, accepted, and free to express their true selves. Through my love, understanding, and support, I teach them that their individuality is a precious gift from God and that being true to themselves is a path to joy and fulfillment. In this nurturing environment, I empower them to embrace their authenticity, to shine brightly in their own unique way, and to carry the light of God's love with them as they navigate the world.

I find ways to make my partner smile every day.

PROVERBS 5:18-19 (ESV)

"LET YOUR FOUNTAIN BE BLESSED, AND REJOICE IN THE WIFE OF YOUR YOUTH, A LOVELY DEER, A GRACEFUL DOE. LET HER BREASTS FILL YOU AT ALL TIMES WITH DELIGHT; BE INTOXICATED ALWAYS IN HER LOVE."

I am committed to finding ways to make my partner smile every day. Whether it's a warm embrace, a heartfelt compliment, or a simple gesture of love, I understand that these everyday moments are the threads that weave the tapestry of our beautiful and timeless love story.

By consistently seeking ways to bring a smile to my partner's face, I lead the charge to create a marriage filled with joy, appreciation, and a deep sense of connection. In this journey of love, I am inspired by the divine example of God's love for us, and I strive to reflect that love in every sweet and tender moment we share.

I look for ways to make my partner's life easier.

SONG OF SOLOMON 4:9 (ESV)

"YOU HAVE CAPTIVATED MY HEART, MY SISTER, MY BRIDE; YOU HAVE CAPTIVATED MY HEART WITH ONE GLANCE OF YOUR EYES, WITH ONE JEWEL OF YOUR NECKLACE."

I know that this practice cultivates selflessness and grace in our home. I believe that by extending acts of kindness and support to my spouse, I mirror God's divine example. Whether it's assisting with daily tasks, offering a listening ear, or simply being a source of comfort, I understand that these gestures of love transform our relationship into a haven of trust and mutual care.

I choose to cultivate love, compassion, and empathy in our relationship.

1 CORINTHIANS 16:14 (NASB1995)

"LET ALL THAT YOU DO BE DONE IN LOVE."

I consciously choose to focus on fostering positive emotions and qualities that contribute to a healthy and thriving marriage. By choosing to cultivate love, compassion, and empathy, I work with my spouse to create an environment of understanding, support, and kindness.

This also encourages me to approach my partner with empathy, seeking to understand their perspective and offering them support and care in times of need. Remembering to lead with love is one of the ways that I elevate my relationship and connection with my partner. I will make this my main priority every day, starting now.

I am dedicated to nurturing our relationship and prioritizing its growth.

LUKE 13:19 (NIV)

"IT IS LIKE A MUSTARD SEED, WHICH A MAN TOOK AND PLANTED IN HIS GARDEN. IT GREW AND BECAME A TREE, AND THE BIRDS PERCHED IN ITS BRANCHES."

I know that working on my marriage is like tending to a garden. It is something that must be consistently planted, watered, and tilled. I cannot expect to see beautiful fruit without laboring and toiling.

It is important that I invest time, effort, attention, care, and energy into the relationship. By dedicating myself to nurturing my relationship and making it a priority, I am creating a sense of commitment and willingness to work through challenges together.

I model the behavior I want to see in my personal relationships because I understand that it starts with me.

JOHN 13:15 (NIV)

"I HAVE SET YOU AN EXAMPLE THAT YOU SHOULD DO AS I HAVE DONE FOR YOU."

I wholeheartedly embrace the principle of modeling the behavior I want to see from my partner. Just as God's love is a shining example of patience, understanding, and grace, I know that by embodying these qualities, I pave the way for a harmonious and loving relationship with my spouse.

I understand that change begins within and that my actions and attitudes can inspire transformation in our partnership. By leading with love, kindness, and the willingness to grow, I set the stage for mutual growth, fostering a home where love and respect flourish. In this sacred endeavor, I draw inspiration from the divine teachings of the Bible, recognizing that it is through my actions that we reflect God's love and grace in our family life.

I tell my family that I love and appreciate them daily.

PROVERBS 20:6-7 (ESV)

"MANY A MAN PROCLAIMS HIS OWN STEADFAST LOVE, BUT A FAITHFUL MAN WHO CAN FIND? THE RIGHTEOUS WHO WALKS IN HIS INTEGRITY—BLESSED ARE HIS CHILDREN AFTER HIM!"

In the beautiful tapestry of family life, I hold the precious tradition of expressing my love and appreciation to my family members daily. I know that showering my loved ones with affection and gratitude on a regular basis is one of the ways I can embody the love and grace that God has called me to.

Through heartfelt words and genuine gestures, I ensure that they know how deeply cherished and valued they are. I understand that these simple yet profound acts of love create a nurturing environment where relationships flourish and where God's love shines brightly. In this daily practice, I am inspired by the divine example of love found in the teachings of the Bible, reinforcing the importance of love, appreciation, and the blessings of family in my life.

I express interest in my partner's hobbies and favorite things, even if they are not naturally appealing to me.

EPHESIANS 5:22-33 (ESV)

"WIVES, SUBMIT TO YOUR OWN HUSBANDS, AS TO THE LORD. FOR THE HUSBAND IS THE HEAD OF THE WIFE EVEN AS CHRIST IS THE HEAD OF THE CHURCH, HIS BODY, AND IS HIMSELF ITS SAVIOR. NOW AS THE CHURCH SUBMITS TO CHRIST, SO ALSO WIVES SHOULD SUBMIT IN EVERYTHING TO THEIR HUSBANDS. HUSBANDS, LOVE YOUR WIVES, AS CHRIST LOVED THE CHURCH AND GAVE HIMSELF UP FOR HER, THAT HE MIGHT SANCTIFY HER, HAVING CLEANSED HER BY THE WASHING OF WATER WITH THE WORD."

I express genuine interest in my partner's hobbies and interests, even when they may not naturally align with my own. Just as God's love for us is boundless and accepting, I believe in fostering a boundless environment of understanding, respect, and unity in our relationship.

By demonstrating a willingness to explore and appreciate the passions and activities that bring joy to my partner, I strengthen the connection and deepen our sense of intimacy. I understand that love is not only about words but also about actions that convey the message, "I value and cherish you for who you are." In this loving endeavor, I find inspiration in the divine example of love as outlined in the Bible, where selflessness and unity are celebrated as the foundations of a strong and harmonious partnership.

I speak positively about my family to others.

PROVERBS 21:9 (ESV)

"IT IS BETTER TO LIVE IN A CORNER OF THE HOUSETOP THAN IN A HOUSE SHARED WITH A QUARRELSOME WIFE."

I vow to always speak positively about my loved ones to others because I know that my words carry power. Just as God's love for us is exemplified by grace and unconditional acceptance, I believe in creating an atmosphere of love, respect, and appreciation within our family circle.

By choosing to share the beautiful moments and virtues of my family when speaking to others, I not only uplift their spirits but also reinforce the bond of trust and unity within our family. I understand that words have the power to shape perceptions and emotions, and I am dedicated to using that power to build and celebrate the love that surrounds us. I am inspired by the divine example of love found in the teachings of the Bible, which remind us to honor and cherish our family as a gift from God.

I do not punish my partner for making mistakes.

MARK 11:25 (ESV)

"AND WHENEVER YOU STAND PRAYING, FORGIVE, IF YOU HAVE ANYTHING AGAINST ANYONE, SO THAT YOUR FATHER ALSO WHO IS IN HEAVEN MAY FORGIVE YOU YOUR TRESPASSES."

I know that God's love for us is characterized by grace, forgiveness, and understanding. I am committed to fostering an environment of compassion and growth within my marriage. I understand that, as humans, we are all prone to making errors, and it is through these mistakes that we learn, evolve, and become better versions of ourselves.

Instead of punishment, I choose to offer support, forgiveness, and a safe space for my partner to learn from their missteps. In this way, we cultivate a relationship built on love, trust, and the understanding that we are on this journey of life and love together, guided by the divine teachings of the Bible.

I extend grace to myself and others in situations that frustrate me.

ROMANS 5:1-5 (NIV)

"THEREFORE, SINCE WE HAVE BEEN JUSTIFIED BY FAITH, WE HAVE PEACE WITH GOD THROUGH OUR LORD JESUS CHRIST. THROUGH HIM WE HAVE ALSO OBTAINED ACCESS BY FAITH INTO THIS GRACE IN WHICH WE STAND, AND WE REJOICE IN HOPE OF THE GLORY OF GOD. NOT ONLY THAT, BUT WE REJOICE IN OUR SUFFERINGS, KNOWING THAT SUFFERING PRODUCES ENDURANCE, AND ENDURANCE PRODUCES CHARACTER, AND CHARACTER PRODUCES HOPE, AND HOPE DOES NOT PUT US TO SHAME, BECAUSE GOD'S LOVE HAS BEEN POURED INTO OUR HEARTS THROUGH THE HOLY SPIRIT WHO HAS BEEN GIVEN TO US."

I commit to extending grace to myself and others in situations that may bring frustration. I understand that we all have moments of frustration and imperfection, but it is through the extension of grace that we nurture growth and unity. By recognizing our shared humanity and embracing grace, we create a haven where love, patience, and understanding prevail.

In this endeavor, I find inspiration in the divine example of grace as found in the teachings of the Bible, which remind us to forgive as we have been forgiven and to love one another as God loves us.

My family is blessed; we find God's divine favor wherever we go.

LUKE 6:38 (NIV)

"GIVE, AND IT WILL BE GIVEN TO YOU. A GOOD MEASURE, PRESSED DOWN, SHAKEN TOGETHER AND RUNNING OVER, WILL BE POURED INTO YOUR LAP. FOR WITH THE MEASURE YOU USE, IT WILL BE MEASURED TO YOU."

My family is divinely blessed, and we are recipients of God's abundant favor. The Bible tells us that God's favor surrounds the righteous; our lives are a testament to His love and grace. With gratitude in our hearts, we embark on each day with the knowledge that we are under His divine protection and guidance.

My faith in His favor strengthens my familial bonds and fills our lives with joy, love, and an enduring sense of purpose. I understand that in His favor, I find the strength to overcome challenges, the wisdom to make sound decisions, and the love to share with one another and those I and my family will encounter on our journey.

My family and I support and uplift one another.

GALATIANS 6:2 (NIV)

"CARRY EACH OTHER'S BURDENS, AND IN THIS WAY, YOU WILL FULFILL THE LAW OF CHRIST."

I know that God, in His Word, calls us to help and support one another. I also know that this is at the heart of strengthening my family's bond. By sharing each other's burdens and offering support, we live out the teachings of Christ and conduct ourselves in the way that He intended.

In my family, we stand side by side, ready to provide a helping hand, a listening ear, and unwavering love in times of both joy and challenge.

I prioritize and value quality time with my loved ones.

PROVERBS 27:9 (NIV)

"PERFUME AND INCENSE BRING JOY TO THE HEART, AND THE PLEASANTNESS OF A FRIEND SPRINGS FROM THEIR HEARTFELT ADVICE."

I know that there are few things as precious as the moments spent with loved ones. Each passing day brings its own demands, but amid it all, I find solace and joy in the embrace of family and friends. My faith teaches me that love is the greatest commandment, and by prioritizing and valuing quality time with loved ones, this divine calling manifests.

These moments of togetherness become the cornerstone of my bonds, the laughter that fills my heart, and the memories that sustain me through life's challenges. In cherishing these moments, I strengthen my relationships and honor the love that God has bestowed upon us, for it is in these moments that I truly experience the fullness of His grace and blessings.

I love my partner enough to have difficult conversations because I know that it's for our growth and betterment.

EPHESIANS 4:15 (NIV)

"INSTEAD, SPEAKING THE TRUTH IN LOVE, WE WILL GROW TO BECOME IN EVERY RESPECT THE MATURE BODY OF HIM WHO IS THE HEAD, THAT IS, CHRIST."

I know that my marriage is like a beautiful tapestry of love and partnership, and the threads of communication are woven with gentle words and courageous conversations. I am willing to engage in difficult dialogues, for it is in these moments of vulnerability and honesty that my partner and I find the fertile ground for growth and betterment.

Love isn't just in laughter and shared joys; it's also in the willingness to address challenges, to listen, to understand, and to work together to strengthen the bond we share. In these moments, I honor the divine gift of love, recognizing that it calls us to be our best selves and to support each other's growth on this remarkable journey of life and love.

I invest in creating new memories with my partner.

PSALM 133:1 (NIV)

"A SONG OF ASCENTS. OF DAVID. HOW GOOD AND PLEASANT IT IS WHEN GOD'S PEOPLE LIVE TOGETHER IN UNITY!"

As my spouse and I invest in creating new memories together, we honor the divine gift of companionship that God has bestowed upon us. These moments of togetherness, whether simple or grand, serve as the building blocks of a lasting bond. They are the chapters in the story of our love, written with laughter, tenderness, and a shared sense of adventure. In these moments, we not only nurture our connection but also express gratitude for the gift of love that continues to blossom and flourish with each memory we create.

I affirm and validate my partner's physical appearance every morning.

1 THESSALONIANS 5:11 (NIV)

"THEREFORE ENCOURAGE ONE ANOTHER AND BUILD EACH OTHER UP, JUST AS IN FACT YOU ARE DOING."

I am dedicated to beginning each day with love and affirmation for my partner. As I wake up beside my beloved spouse, I know that I have the power to uplift their spirit and reinforce their sense of self-worth. I love being the first person they see and letting my lips utter the first words they hear every day. Affirming and validating my partner's physical appearance each morning is not just a simple act of kindness; it's a testament to my commitment to love them unconditionally.

In these moments, I mirror God's love, appreciating the beauty and uniqueness that each day brings. My words become a source of strength and encouragement, creating an atmosphere of love and acceptance in our home. In the warm embrace of our affirmations, we build a foundation of love that stands firm against the challenges of life. I get joy in reminding my partner that they are cherished, valued, and endlessly adored.

I teach my children the importance of self-love and self-acceptance.

EPHESIANS 6:4 (ESV)

"FATHERS, DO NOT PROVOKE YOUR CHILDREN TO ANGER, BUT BRING THEM UP IN THE DISCIPLINE AND INSTRUCTION OF THE LORD."

Teaching my children the importance of self-love and self-acceptance is one of the greatest gifts I can give them in their journey through life. My partner and I instill in our children the knowledge that they are fearfully and wonderfully made in God's image. I guide them to embrace their unique qualities, strengths, and quirks, helping them understand that true beauty and worth come from within.

By nurturing their self-love, I empower them to face life's challenges with resilience and grace. I show them that self-acceptance is the cornerstone of strong self-esteem and healthy relationships. Through our example and encouragement, I equip my children to radiate God's love from the inside out, knowing they are cherished just as they are.

I do not expect my partner to be a mind reader.

HEBREWS 10:24-25 (NIV)

"AND LET US CONSIDER HOW WE MAY SPUR ONE ANOTHER ON TOWARD LOVE AND GOOD DEEDS, NOT GIVING UP MEETING TOGETHER, AS SOME ARE IN THE HABIT OF DOING, BUT ENCOURAGING ONE ANOTHER—AND ALL THE MORE AS YOU SEE THE DAY APPROACHING."

I understand that expecting my partner to be a mind reader is unrealistic and unfair. Instead, I embrace open and honest communication as the cornerstone of our relationship. I express my thoughts, desires, and needs with clarity and kindness, knowing that my partner can better understand and support me when I share my heart openly.

I am receptive to their words, listening with love and empathy. Through this mutual respect and communication, our love deepens, and our connection grows stronger. In the gentle art of understanding, I find harmony and unity, nurturing a love that is steadfast and enduring.

I keep my word with my family members, I do not make promises I can't keep.

PROVERBS 25:14 (NIV)

"LIKE CLOUDS AND WIND WITHOUT RAIN, IS ONE WHO BOASTS OF GIFTS NEVER GIVEN."

In my family, integrity, and trust are the building blocks of our relationships. I hold steadfast to the principle of keeping my word with my loved ones. I understand that promises are not made lightly; they are sacred commitments that hold the power to make or break the bonds of love and trust. By being true to my word, I demonstrate my reliability and show deep respect for the faith my family places in me.

I recognize that keeping promises, no matter how small or significant, is a testament to my love and dedication to them. I cultivate an environment of honesty, love, and security where we can rely on each other wholeheartedly, knowing that our words are as good as our deeds.

Let your Life be affirmed

June:

Career and Finances

Mastering the Art of Stewardship

We spend more time at work than we do at home. Where we choose to work, and the type of career that we choose plays a crucial role in our overall wellbeing and satisfaction with life.

Having a career that aligns with your passion and purpose is a profound blessing. It allows you to wake up every day with a sense of fulfillment and confidence, knowing that you're walking in God's plan for your life.

Pursuing your passion in your career is not only an act of obedience to His divine calling but also a way to honor the talents and gifts He has bestowed upon you. It empowers you not only spiritually but also financially, enabling you to provide for your family's needs as God's Word commands.

As you walk in your purpose and manage your finances wisely, you become a faithful steward of the resources God has entrusted to you, setting a strong example for your loved ones, and ensuring that you can support them in their journey of faith and purpose as well.

I am a wise planner of my finances.

PROVERBS 21:20 (NIV)

"THE WISE STORE UP CHOICE FOOD AND OLIVE OIL, BUT FOOLS GULP THEIRS DOWN."

I know that God wants me to be a prudent manager of my personal finances. I understand that this is not just a matter of earthly wisdom but also a reflection of my faith. It's about recognizing that the resources I have are entrusted to me by God.

When I am a wise planner of my finances, I honor God's provision and demonstrate good stewardship. I create a stable foundation for my family, allowing me to support their needs and fulfill my God-given responsibilities. Financial prudence isn't just about accumulating wealth; it's about using my resources in a way that aligns with my values and priorities, ensuring that my financial decisions reflect the principles of faith, responsibility, and generosity that are deeply rooted in my Christian beliefs.

Unexpected money finds me.

PSALM 37:4 (NIV)

"TAKE DELIGHT IN THE LORD, AND HE WILL GIVE YOU THE DESIRES OF YOUR HEART."

I walk in financial abundance and boldly declare my faith. I believe that God's blessings can come in unexpected ways, including through financial provision. By having faith and being a responsible steward of my resources, I open myself to the divine flow of abundance. This belief is not rooted in materialism but in the understanding that God cares for His children and provides for their needs. It encourages me to trust God's timing and grace in all aspects of my life, including my finances, knowing that He is the ultimate source of my blessings.

I find charitable organizations and worthy causes to donate to.

ACTS 20:35 (ESV)

"IN ALL THINGS I HAVE SHOWN YOU THAT BY WORKING HARD IN THIS WAY WE MUST HELP THE WEAK AND REMEMBER THE WORDS OF THE LORD JESUS, HOW HE HIMSELF SAID, 'IT IS MORE BLESSED TO GIVE THAN TO RECEIVE.'"

I know that God has blessed me to be a blessing. I know that He has provided me with the resources to give to those who are in need. I understand that charitable donations and philanthropic pursuits are not mere acts of generosity; they are tangible expressions of God's love and compassion.

My faith calls me to love my neighbors as I love myself and to care for those in need. Giving to charitable causes and organizations aligns with these principles and pleases God because it reflects His heart for the less fortunate.

When I use my financial resources to make a positive impact on the lives of others, I become a vessel of God's grace and blessings in the world. It's a way of sharing God's love and abundance with those who may be struggling. Moreover, as I give, I also receive a sense of fulfillment and purpose, knowing that I am making a difference in the lives of those who need it most. Charitable giving is more than a responsibility; it's a privilege and an opportunity to be God's hands and feet in the world.

I show grace to my colleagues and staff members, even when I feel they don't deserve it.

TITUS 2:11-12 (NIV)

"FOR THE GRACE OF GOD HAS APPEARED THAT OFFERS SALVATION TO ALL PEOPLE.

It teaches us to say "No" to ungodliness and worldly passions, and to live self-controlled, upright and godly lives in this present age."

I know that it is important to show grace to the people I work with. This not only creates a harmonious workplace but also aligns with Christian principles. I know that God has called me to show grace and extend love to others in all aspects of my life, including my professional relationships.

By fostering an atmosphere of understanding and support, I actively improve my work environment while demonstrating Christ's love in action.

Showing grace to my colleagues means being patient, forgiving, and compassionate, even in challenging situations. It's about being a team player, valuing my colleagues' contributions, and striving for unity. I create a workplace that reflects the values I hold dear as a believer and become a beacon of God's love in the business world.

I am deeply grateful for the fruits of my labor.

PSALM 128:2 (ESV)

"YOU SHALL EAT THE FRUIT OF THE LABOR OF YOUR HANDS; YOU SHALL BE BLESSED, AND IT SHALL BE WELL WITH YOU."

I know that it's essential to take a moment to enjoy the fruits of my labor and celebrate the blessings that come from my efforts. As a Christian, I am called to be grateful for the opportunity to earn a living and provide for my family.

Each day of work is an additional chance to honor God by using my talents and abilities to make a positive impact and contribute to the wellbeing of my loved ones. By holding deep gratitude for my work and the abundance it brings, I will find joy in the provision it offers and the richness it adds to my life. It's a reminder that my efforts are not in vain, and through faith and diligence, I can (and will) create a better future for myself and those I care for.

I am included in lucrative contracts and deals that increase and enhance my business and financial success.

PROVERBS 14:23 (ESV)

"IN ALL TOIL THERE IS PROFIT, BUT MERE TALK TENDS ONLY TO POVERTY."

I know that through faith, determination, and investing in the right connections, I will attract lucrative contracts and deals that will not only increase my business success but also enhance my financial wellbeing. I trust that God has a plan for my career and financial journey, and these opportunities are part of His divine provision.

By staying focused, working diligently, and maintaining a positive mindset, I open the door for abundant blessings in my professional life. With God's guidance and my unwavering faith, I am confident that these opportunities will come to fruition, leading to greater success and prosperity.

I take the time to ensure that my business is established properly.

1 CORINTHIANS 14:40 (KJV)

"LET ALL THINGS BE DONE DECENTLY AND IN ORDER."

I know and understand the importance of doing things decently and in order, especially when it comes to setting up and establishing my business. This includes making sure that the foundation of the business is solid, which involves setting up a separate business bank account to maintain financial clarity and responsibility. Additionally, it's crucial I adhere to government tax requirements and legal obligations specific to my type of business structure, whether it's a sole proprietorship, limited liability corporation (LLC), or corporation.

By investing time, energy, and resources to ensure that my business is established properly, I not only honor God's principles of order but also create a firm foundation for success and growth, allowing me to fulfill my purpose and positively impact others.

I establish my budget and stick to it.

LUKE 14:28 (NIV)

"SUPPOSE ONE OF YOU WANTS TO BUILD A TOWER. WON'T YOU FIRST SIT DOWN AND ESTIMATE THE COST TO SEE IF YOU HAVE ENOUGH MONEY TO COMPLETE IT?"

I know that budgeting is a fundamental aspect of responsible financial stewardship, and it aligns with the principles of order and wise management that I believe in. Creating and adhering to a budget helps me and my family honor God with our finances by allocating resources intentionally, planning for the future, and avoiding financial stress.

I understand that budgeting is a practical tool that empowers me to make informed decisions about spending, saving, and giving, leading to financial peace and the ability to live a life in alignment with my values and priorities. Through budgeting, I manage my money wisely and ensure that I have the means to support my loved ones and give back to my community as part of my Christian faith. I know that applying discipline in my money management will ultimately bless me and place me in a position to bless others. Today, I commit to being an excellent steward of my finances!

My name is in rooms where major deals are happening.

ECCLESIASTES 5:19 (NLT)

"AND IT IS A GOOD THING TO RECEIVE WEALTH FROM GOD AND THE GOOD HEALTH TO ENJOY IT. TO ENJOY YOUR WORK AND ACCEPT YOUR LOT IN LIFE—THIS IS INDEED A GIFT FROM GOD."

I speak blessings and favor in my business daily. I am thankful for the divine connections that God sends my way. I know that God's favor opens doors that no one else can. I seek His guidance and align my actions with His principles, therefore positioning myself for success in business.

It's not about who I know but who knows *me*! I trust in God's favor, and my name is mentioned in rooms where major deals are happening! Opportunities flow to me!

My success is a testament to God's provision and His desire for me to prosper as His faithful steward. By nurturing my relationship with Him and practicing integrity, I will attract and obtain contracts and financial success that not only benefit me but allow me to make a positive impact on my community and those I serve.

I delight in gifting people anonymously; I know this is one of the many ways I can do the work of God.

MATTHEW 6:3-4 (NIV)

"BUT WHEN YOU GIVE TO THE NEEDY, DO NOT LET YOUR LEFT HAND KNOW WHAT YOUR RIGHT HAND IS DOING, SO THAT YOUR GIVING MAY BE IN SECRET. THEN YOUR FATHER, WHO SEES WHAT IS DONE IN SECRET, WILL REWARD YOU."

I know that giving anonymously is a beautiful way to emulate God's love and grace in the lives of others. I know that these acts of kindness, done without expecting anything in return, align with God's teachings. I don't give to receive attention or accolades. I give because God has planted the desire to be a blessing deep in my heart and soul. This desire to give is woven intricately into the fabric of who I am.

When I give selflessly and anonymously, I know that I am doing the work of God, spreading love and light where it is needed the most. It's a powerful way to make a positive impact and inspire others to do the same, all while humbly serving as vessels of God's love.

I pray and ask God before making business decisions and selecting business partners.

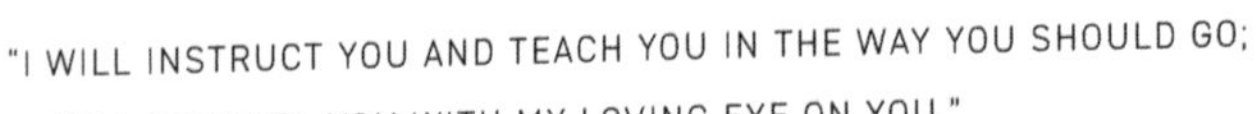

PSALM 32:8 (NIV)

"I WILL INSTRUCT YOU AND TEACH YOU IN THE WAY YOU SHOULD GO; I WILL COUNSEL YOU WITH MY LOVING EYE ON YOU."

I know that praying and seeking God's guidance before making business decisions and choosing business partners is a practice rooted in faith and wisdom. I acknowledge the importance of aligning my business endeavors with God's will.

When I include God in my business decisions, I show Him that I am surrendered to His divine plan. I am also trusting that He will lead me on a path of righteousness and success. It's a powerful way to navigate the challenges of entrepreneurship, ensuring that my choices are in line with my faith and values.

I teach my children the principles of financial responsibility and wealth management.

PROVERBS 13:22 (NIV)

"A GOOD PERSON LEAVES AN INHERITANCE FOR THEIR CHILDREN'S CHILDREN, BUT A SINNER'S WEALTH IS STORED UP FOR THE RIGHTEOUS."

I know that teaching my children the principles of financial responsibility and wealth management is a gift that keeps on giving. I impart not only the practical aspects of managing money wisely but also the importance of aligning my financial decisions with God's principles.

By teaching my children to be responsible stewards of their resources and to manage wealth with integrity and generosity, I give them valuable tools to secure their financial future and nurture their spiritual growth. I understand that this teaching is an investment in their fiduciary wellbeing and a legacy of faithfulness for my children's children.

I am a thought leader in my field, and people pay me well for my valuable business insights.

PROVERBS 24:14 (NIV)

"KNOW ALSO THAT WISDOM IS LIKE HONEY FOR YOU: IF YOU FIND IT, THERE IS A FUTURE HOPE FOR YOU, AND YOUR HOPE WILL NOT BE CUT OFF."

I am a beacon of wisdom and insight in my field. My expertise creates a high demand for my niche knowledge. I believe that God has blessed me with valuable knowledge and insights, and I am committed to sharing that wisdom to help others succeed in their business endeavors.

When people seek my guidance and are willing to invest in the wisdom I offer, it's not just a transaction; it's a mutual journey toward growth, prosperity, and fulfilling God's purpose for their lives.

I am not consumed by the appeal of material things.

1 TIMOTHY 6:7 (NIV)

"FOR WE BROUGHT NOTHING INTO THE WORLD, AND WE CAN TAKE NOTHING OUT OF IT."

I understand that I live in a world often consumed by the allure of material possessions. I do not subscribe to society's obsession with consumption and greed. I stand as a steadfast example that true abundance comes from within and through my connection with God. I draw inspiration from God's Word, which reminds me that material wealth is temporary, but my spiritual growth and connection with God are eternal.

I am not consumed by material things; instead, I seek the richness of faith, love, and meaningful relationships. These are the treasures that truly endure and bring fulfillment in this life and the next.

I walk in financial freedom and find ways to help others do the same.

GALATIANS 5:13 (NIV)

"YOU, MY BROTHERS AND SISTERS, WERE CALLED TO BE FREE. BUT DO NOT USE YOUR FREEDOM TO INDULGE THE FLESH; RATHER, SERVE ONE ANOTHER HUMBLY IN LOVE."

I know that financial freedom is not just about wealth; it's about stewardship and service to others. As God clearly outlines in His Word, I understand that by walking in financial freedom, I can better serve others and inspire them to achieve the same.

My goal is not just personal success but to be a guiding light, showing others the path to financial liberation through wise management and generosity.

This reflects God's love and grace, and it is through this journey that I uplift and empower my family and friends.

I intentionally support small businesses because I know that has a positive impact on my local economy and community.

PROVERBS 3:27 (NIV)

"DO NOT WITHHOLD GOOD FROM THOSE TO WHOM IT IS DUE WHEN IT IS IN YOUR POWER TO ACT."

I consciously choose to support small businesses because it aligns with the principles of community and stewardship that I hold dear. By supporting small businesses, I use my resources to contribute to the local economy and foster a sense of togetherness and mutual support within my community.

Patronizing and supporting small businesses is a tangible way to live out the Christian values of unity and service. I affirm these businesses, helping them achieve their dreams while building a stronger, more interconnected community.

My business idea is a blessing, and I will take steps today to bring it to fruition.

PROVERBS 16:3 (NIV)

"COMMIT TO THE LORD WHATEVER YOU DO, AND HE WILL ESTABLISH YOUR PLANS."

I declare and boldly believe that my business idea is a divine blessing. I'm committed to taking purposeful steps every day to manifest it.

I know that through faith and diligent effort, God's guidance will lead me to success in this endeavor. This belief fuels my determination and empowers me to inspire others to pursue their God-given visions and turn them into tangible blessings for themselves and their families.

My faith cultivates a healthy and positive work environment.

COLOSSIANS 3:23 (NIV)

"WHATEVER YOU DO, WORK AT IT WITH ALL YOUR HEART, AS WORKING FOR THE LORD, NOT FOR HUMAN MASTERS."

My unwavering faith serves as the cornerstone of the positive and thriving work environment I create. I draw inspiration from God's Word, and I strive to be a positive light to those I work with.

I lead by example, infusing each day with positive energy, dedication, respect, and love. This enhances productivity and fosters a culture of mutual support where everyone can flourish personally and professionally.

My faith guides me to uplift and encourage my team, helping them recognize their God-given potential and excel in their roles. This cultivates much more than just a job; it creates a safe space where employees can strengthen their careers while nourishing their overall wellbeing and life satisfaction.

I am trusted by God to manage great wealth, and I use my wealth to create radical positive change in my life and the lives of others.

PROVERBS 11:25 (NIV)

"A GENEROUS PERSON WILL PROSPER; WHOEVER REFRESHES OTHERS WILL BE REFRESHED."

I know that God has entrusted me with great wealth, not for my own interests, but to create radical positive change in my life and the lives of others. I embrace this truth wholeheartedly, understanding that my wealth is a divine tool for making a significant impact in the world.

With unwavering faith and a heart full of gratitude, I seek opportunities to support causes close to my heart, uplift those in need, and contribute to the betterment of my community and beyond. This is more than a responsibility; it is a blessing, and I approach it with reverence and purpose.

I am productive, purposeful, and profitable.

PROVERBS 3:9-10 (NLT)

"HONOR THE LORD WITH YOUR WEALTH AND WITH THE BEST PART OF EVERYTHING YOU PRODUCE. THEN HE WILL FILL YOUR BARNS WITH GRAIN, AND YOUR VATS WILL OVERFLOW WITH GOOD WINE."

I know that God has called me to be productive, to ensure my words, thoughts, and actions are purposeful, and to work so that my business endeavors are profitable. He calls me to do this by aligning my actions with His divine plan for my life.

With this calling in mind, I approach every task and endeavor with diligence, knowing that my efforts are part of a greater purpose. Through God's grace and my unfaltering faith in His promises, I am productive and purpose-driven, ensuring that each action I take contributes to a life filled with abundance and blessings.

As I walk this path, I trust in God's provision and guidance, embracing the promise of prosperity that aligns with His divine will.

I adopt an abundance mindset in my career and personal finances.

PHILIPPIANS 4:19 (NIV)

"AND MY GOD WILL MEET ALL YOUR NEEDS ACCORDING TO THE RICHES OF HIS GLORY IN CHRIST JESUS."

I release lack and walk in total abundance in both my career and personal finances. This transformative mindset is rooted in my faith and total trust in God's Word.

God's Word reminds and reassures me that His abundance knows no bounds. I carry this truth into every aspect of my life. I know that there is more than enough for everyone, and as I embrace this mindset, I allow it to frame my thoughts and govern my actions.

I am open to the limitless possibilities that God's blessings bring. With gratitude and faith, I release scarcity thinking, knowing that God's abundance is my birthright. I am destined for financial and career success that aligns with His divine plan.

I actively give my time, energy, and resources to enhance the community that I live in.

1 TIMOTHY 6:17-19 (NIV)

"COMMAND THOSE WHO ARE RICH IN THIS PRESENT WORLD NOT TO BE ARROGANT NOR TO PUT THEIR HOPE IN WEALTH, WHICH IS SO UNCERTAIN, BUT TO PUT THEIR HOPE IN GOD, WHO RICHLY PROVIDES US WITH EVERYTHING FOR OUR ENJOYMENT. COMMAND THEM TO DO GOOD, TO BE RICH IN GOOD DEEDS, AND TO BE GENEROUS AND WILLING TO SHARE. IN THIS WAY, THEY WILL LAY UP TREASURE FOR THEMSELVES AS A FIRM FOUNDATION FOR THE COMING AGE, SO THAT THEY MAY TAKE HOLD OF THE LIFE THAT IS TRULY LIFE."

I take great pride and pleasure in actively contributing to the betterment of my community. I know that this reflects my faith and values as a believer. God's Word reminds me of the importance of selflessly supporting and uplifting those around me.

By giving my time, energy, and resources to enhance my community, I am living out the principles of love, compassion, and service that Christ taught. I understand that when we come together to support one another, we create a stronger and more vibrant community, which in turn reflects the love of God. It's not just a duty but a privilege to make a positive impact, and I do so with joy, knowing that my actions align with God's plan for a better world.

I positively impact lives by creating jobs with my successful business.

1 THESSALONIANS 5:11 (NIV)

"THEREFORE ENCOURAGE ONE ANOTHER AND BUILD EACH OTHER UP, JUST AS IN FACT YOU ARE DOING."

I know that being an entrepreneur holds a greater purpose and can benefit my surrounding community. Creating jobs through my business is a tangible way of spreading God's love and blessings to those around me.

I know that through my diligence and dedication, I not only achieve success in my business but also have the opportunity to positively impact the lives of others. By providing jobs, I contribute to the financial well-being of individuals and their families, enabling them to fulfill their own dreams and aspirations.

I consider it a privilege and a high calling to be a conduit of God's blessings. I embrace this responsibility with gratitude, knowing that my business is a means to make a meaningful difference in the world.

I am honest and operate with integrity at my job/in my business.

PROVERBS 10:9 (NIV)

"WHOEVER WALKS IN INTEGRITY WALKS SECURELY, BUT WHOEVER TAKES CROOKED PATHS WILL BE FOUND OUT."

I know that operating with honesty and integrity in my job or business is not only a personal choice but a reflection of my commitment to living a Christ-centered life.

God's Word serves as a constant reminder that honesty and integrity are virtues and sources of strength and security. By adhering to these principles, I gain the trust of my colleagues, clients, and partners while aligning myself with God's divine plan for my life.

I recognize that my actions in my professional life are an opportunity to bear witness to His grace and love, and I strive daily to honor that calling through my honest and principled conduct.

I am grateful for income and the means to meet my financial obligations.

1 TIMOTHY 6:6 (NIV)

"BUT GODLINESS WITH CONTENTMENT IS GREAT GAIN."

I express deep and sincere gratitude for the income and resources I have. This expression of gratitude has become a truly meaningful ritual that I look forward to every day.

In His Word, God emphasizes the importance of contentment and gratitude in my financial life. By being grateful for the income and means to meet my financial obligations, I align myself with God's desire for us to be content with what we have.

I understand that my gratitude is a way of acknowledging God's provision and a source of peace and contentment in my life. It also allows me to approach financial challenges with faith and resilience, knowing that God's blessings are abundant and that I can navigate any situation with His grace.

I look for ways to hone my craft and improve my professional skill set.

PROVERBS 22:29 (NIV)

"DO YOU SEE SOMEONE SKILLED IN THEIR WORK? THEY WILL SERVE BEFORE KINGS; THEY WILL NOT SERVE BEFORE OFFICIALS OF LOW RANK."

I am dedicated to seeking continuous improvement in my professional skills. I commit to this practice as a reflection of my dedication to properly stewarding the talents and gifts that God has bestowed upon me.

I recognize God's gentle nudges highlighting the significance of skill and excellence in my endeavors. I know that He calls me to be at my best. By honing my craft and improving my skills, I position myself to serve in more significant capacities and impact my community and workplace positively.

I know that God's Word is a reminder that my commitment to growth and excellence can open doors to greater opportunities and allow me to fulfill my God-given purpose more effectively.

My career is in alignment with my personal values and beliefs.

PROVERBS 24:27 (ESV)

"PREPARE YOUR WORK OUTSIDE; GET EVERYTHING READY FOR YOURSELF IN THE FIELD, AND AFTER THAT BUILD YOUR HOUSE."

I understand that aligning my career with my personal values and beliefs is the key to finding true purpose and fulfillment in my work. If I have not already done so, I know that I must choose a career that resonates with my values. By making an aligned career choice, I am more likely to approach my work with passion and dedication, knowing that I am ultimately serving a higher purpose.

This alignment ensures that my career becomes an extension of my faith, allowing me to live out my beliefs through my actions and positively impact those around me. This is a powerful way to find meaning and satisfaction in my professional journey while staying true to my core beliefs and values.

My career allows me to use my God-given gifts and abilities to solve problems and positively impact others.

1 PETER 4:10 (NIV)

"EACH OF YOU SHOULD USE WHATEVER GIFT YOU HAVE RECEIVED TO SERVE OTHERS, AS FAITHFUL STEWARDS OF GOD'S GRACE IN ITS VARIOUS FORMS."

I find great joy in discovering and utilizing my God-given gifts and abilities in my career. This is a source of personal fulfillment and a means to serve a higher purpose.

Having a career that allows me to use my talents and natural abilities enables me to solve problems and make a positive impact. I honor my Creator by using the unique abilities He has given me for the betterment of others and the world around me.

I find ways to inspire and motivate my colleagues and/or staff members.

PROVERBS 15:30 (ESV)

"A CHEERFUL LOOK BRINGS JOY TO THE HEART, AND GOOD NEWS REFRESHES THE BONES."

I look forward to inspiring and motivating my colleagues and/or staff members each day! This is not just about boosting productivity; it's about creating a positive and encouraging work environment where everyone can thrive.

When I inspire and motivate my coworkers, I know that I am contributing to their personal and professional growth while fostering a sense of unity and purpose. This benefits the individual team members, enhances the overall success and harmony of the team, and positively impacts the organization as a whole.

I find healthy and positive ways to cope with the stress that comes with my professional responsibilities.

PHILIPPIANS 4:6-7 (NIV)

"DO NOT BE ANXIOUS ABOUT ANYTHING, BUT IN EVERY SITUATION, BY PRAYER AND PETITION, WITH THANKSGIVING, PRESENT YOUR REQUESTS TO GOD. AND THE PEACE OF GOD, WHICH TRANSCENDS ALL UNDERSTANDING, WILL GUARD YOUR HEARTS AND YOUR MINDS IN CHRIST JESUS."

I know that coping with stress in a healthy and positive way is essential for maintaining my wellbeing and effectiveness in my professional life. By seeking God in prayer and maintaining a thankful heart, I find inner peace and strength to navigate the challenges of my professional responsibilities.

I seek to adopt practices like meditation, exercise, and setting healthy boundaries to further enhance my ability to manage stress in a positive way, allowing me to lead a more fulfilling life and positively impact those around me.

I learn a new lesson from every chapter of my professional life.

PROVERBS 2:6 (NIV)

"FOR THE LORD GIVES WISDOM; FROM HIS MOUTH COMES KNOWLEDGE AND UNDERSTANDING."

In my professional journey, I have encountered various chapters that have shaped my growth and wisdom. As I navigate through each chapter of my career, I know that I have the opportunity to learn valuable lessons, gain knowledge, and deepen my understanding.

These experiences, whether they bring success or challenges, contribute to my personal and professional development. By approaching each chapter with a learning mindset and seeking God's guidance, I can extract wisdom and insights that benefit my career, enrich my life, and enable me to inspire and support others on their journeys. I view my career as an opportunity to use my gifts and talents to earn a living and positively impact others. I walk in this frame of mind daily to help keep me focused and aligned with my purpose.

Let your Life be affirmed

July:

Share Your Gifts and Shine Your Light

Walking Boldly in God's Purpose for Your Gifts and Talents

In the grand story of your life, you were crafted with a unique purpose—a divine calling that resonates within your soul. It is a purpose that beckons you to use your God-given gifts, talents, and experiences to make a positive impact on the world around you.

Your purpose is not a random occurrence but a carefully crafted plan by the Creator. Embracing your purpose aligns you with God's divine blueprint for your life. Within you are untapped gifts waiting to be shared - gifts that have the power to inspire, heal, and uplift. When you use your gifts to serve others, you fulfill your purpose and bring light and hope to a world in need.

Your life experiences, joys and trials, are intricate threads in the tapestry of your purpose. When sharing your story, you offer hope and solace to those who face similar challenges.

When you begin to tap into God's infinite source of wisdom, fulfilling your purpose becomes your guiding star—a true north star that keeps you grounded, focused, and resilient in the face of adversity. Trusting in your divine purpose, you can learn to navigate life's complexities with unshakeable faith.

Your journey isn't just about personal fulfillment; it's about inspiring others to embark on their own path of purpose. By embracing your calling, you become a beacon of light, encouraging those around you to discover and embrace their unique God-given destinies.

This month, double down on your commitment to living a purpose filled life. Each affirmation will explore the profound significance of living a purpose-driven life, nurturing, and sharing your gifts, and using your story to inspire and uplift. As you embark on this transformative journey, you will find that in fulfilling your purpose, you will find yourself and leave an enduring legacy of love, hope, and faith.

I find ways to share my gifts with my network.

ROMANS 12:6 (NIV)

"WE HAVE DIFFERENT GIFTS, ACCORDING TO THE GRACE GIVEN TO EACH OF US."

I understand the importance of sharing my gifts with the people I know. I realize that this is a beautiful way to spread love, positivity, and inspiration to my sphere of influence.

My unique talents and abilities are not meant to be hidden but shared with the world, enriching the lives of those around me. When I generously give of myself, I fulfill my calling and create a ripple effect of kindness and empowerment, strengthening the bonds within my network and uplifting everyone around me.

I know that my voice is valuable.

2 CORINTHIANS 1:3-4 (NIV)

"PRAISE BE TO THE GOD AND FATHER OF OUR LORD JESUS CHRIST, THE FATHER OF COMPASSION AND THE GOD OF ALL COMFORT, WHO COMFORTS US IN ALL OUR TROUBLES, SO THAT WE CAN COMFORT THOSE IN ANY TROUBLE WITH THE COMFORT WE OURSELVES RECEIVE FROM GOD."

My voice is a precious gift from God, and it holds immense value. My voice is not the sound that comes out of my mouth when I speak. It's much deeper than that. My voice embodies my unique perspective, thoughts, and life experiences.

My voice has the power to inspire, uplift, heal, and bring positive change to the lives of those around me. Recognizing the value of my voice means embracing the responsibility to use it for good; to share my wisdom, experiences, and faith to encourage and motivate others on their life journeys. I have the potential to make a significant impact, and my voice is an essential tool in spreading love and light in the world.

I authentically share the messages that God gives me.

MATTHEW 28:19 (KJV)

"GO YE THEREFORE, AND TEACH ALL NATIONS, BAPTIZING THEM IN THE NAME OF THE FATHER, AND OF THE SON, AND OF THE HOLY GHOST."

I listen to God's voice and the important messages He gives me. In these messages, He provides me with important instructions and wisdom that are necessary for me to fulfill the calling He has assigned to me.

When I receive divine messages and insights, it's a testament to the unique gifts and understanding that God has blessed me with. By sharing these messages authentically, I become a channel of God's grace and wisdom to those who need it most. My willingness to be a faithful steward of these messages can have a profound impact on the lives of others, guiding them toward faith, hope, and purpose. I accept and honor this divine responsibility and take great care to spread God's Word faithfully and with an abundance of joy.

I find new and creative avenues to express myself.

EPHESIANS 2:10 (ESV)

"FOR WE ARE HIS WORKMANSHIP, CREATED IN CHRIST JESUS FOR GOOD WORKS, WHICH GOD PREPARED BEFOREHAND, THAT WE SHOULD WALK IN THEM."

I know that self-expression is a divine gift that allows us to connect with our true selves and others on a deeper level. When I prioritize finding new and creative avenues to express myself, I honor the unique way God has fearfully and wonderfully made me.

This self-expression brings me joy and fulfillment while enabling me to touch the hearts and souls of those around me. Through authentic self-expression, I can shine God's light in the world and fulfill the purpose He has set before me while inspiring others to do the same.

I know that my purpose is directly tied to my gifts and talents.

1 TIMOTHY 4:14 (ESV)

"DO NOT NEGLECT THE GIFT YOU HAVE, WHICH WAS GIVEN YOU BY PROPHECY WHEN THE COUNCIL OF ELDERS LAID THEIR HANDS ON YOU."

I know that my purpose is intricately connected to the gifts and talents that God has given me. Recognizing my unique abilities and using them to serve others is one of the keys to living a fulfilling life. I recognize that this is also part of my divine calling.

My gifts are like puzzle pieces that fit perfectly into the grand design of God's plan for my life. I know that by embracing my gifts, I align myself with my purpose fully and allow myself to become an instrument of His love, grace, and change in the world.

I will not sit on my gifts; I know that God has called me to share them.

MATTHEW 5:15-16 (NIV)

"NEITHER DO PEOPLE LIGHT A LAMP AND PUT IT UNDER A BOWL. INSTEAD, THEY PUT IT ON ITS STAND, AND IT GIVES LIGHT TO EVERYONE IN THE HOUSE. IN THE SAME WAY, LET YOUR LIGHT SHINE BEFORE OTHERS, THAT THEY MAY SEE YOUR GOOD DEEDS AND GLORIFY YOUR FATHER IN HEAVEN."

With faith and purpose guiding me, I boldly share my gifts with the world. Just as a lamp is meant to illuminate a room, my gifts are meant to illuminate the lives of those around me.

I consider it a beautiful expression of my faith to use my God-given talents to bring light, hope, and inspiration to others. I recognize that this ultimately glorifies God through my actions and the impact that I make in the world.

I invest time, energy, and resources in perfecting my gifts and talents because I want to offer God my best.

ROMANS 12:6 (ESV)

"HAVING GIFTS THAT DIFFER ACCORDING TO THE GRACE GIVEN TO US, LET US USE THEM: IF PROPHECY, IN PROPORTION TO OUR FAITH."

I know that dedicating myself to perfecting my God-given gifts and talents is a wonderful way to honor my Creator. When I invest my time, energy, and resources in honing my skills and abilities, I do so with the intention of offering God my best.

My commitment to excellence reflects my gratitude for the gifts I have been given. It also allows me to serve others and fulfill my purpose in a way that glorifies God.

I do not allow myself to become distracted from fulfilling my purpose.

2 CORINTHIANS 2:10-11 (NIV)

"ANYONE YOU FORGIVE, I ALSO FORGIVE. AND WHAT I HAVE FORGIVEN—IF THERE WAS ANYTHING TO FORGIVE—I HAVE FORGIVEN IN THE SIGHT OF CHRIST FOR YOUR SAKE, IN ORDER THAT SATAN MIGHT NOT OUTWIT US. FOR WE ARE NOT UNAWARE OF HIS DEVICES."

I know that I must stay focused, avoiding anything that distracts me from fulfilling my purpose. Just as the enemy is wise and knows how to get me off track, I must be wise and aware of how he operates.

I know that staying focused on my purpose is essential in my journey of faith. Distractions will always try to divert me from the path God has set before me. By remaining steadfast and not allowing myself to be swayed by worldly temptations or distractions, I can press on toward my divine calling. God has a unique purpose for my life, and my commitment to staying focused ensures that I continue to walk in His light and fulfill the mission He has entrusted to me.

I am divinely supported and presented with massive opportunities to soar.

PSALM 54:4 (NASB1995)

"BEHOLD, GOD IS MY HELPER; THE LORD IS THE SUSTAINER OF MY SOUL."

I see and feel God's divine support working in my life. His support is a beautiful and awe-inspiring aspect of my faith journey. When I trust in Him and His divine plan, I discover that His support brings countless opportunities into my life.

God's present help is like a steady hand guiding me through the twists and turns of my life's path. With God by my side, I can overcome challenges, achieve my dreams, and find purpose and fulfillment in all that I do. His unwavering love and support remind me that, as a believer, I am never alone. There's no limit to what I can accomplish with His grace. Embracing His divine support is an incredible blessing that fills my life with hope, purpose, and boundless opportunities to shine His light.

I use what I have been through to help someone break through.

PSALM 37:24 (NASB1995)

"WHEN HE FALLS, HE WILL NOT BE HURLED HEADLONG, BECAUSE THE LORD IS THE ONE WHO HOLDS HIS HAND."

My journey through life often leads me down challenging paths, but as a Christian, I am called to use those lessons to help others facing similar trials.

When I extend a helping hand and share my stories of triumph over adversity, I provide comfort and support to those in need and shine a light on the hope and healing that can be found through faith. I create a ripple effect of encouragement and inspiration, reminding others that they are not alone and that there is a way forward, even in the darkest of times.

My purpose is greater than my ego.

PHILIPPIANS 2:3-4 (NIV)

"DO NOTHING OUT OF SELFISH AMBITION OR VAIN CONCEIT. RATHER, IN HUMILITY VALUE OTHERS ABOVE YOURSELVES, NOT LOOKING TO YOUR OWN INTERESTS BUT EACH OF YOU TO THE INTERESTS OF THE OTHERS."

I know that my purpose is what I was sent here to do. I also know that my ego can try to get in the way of my purpose. When I shift my focus from self-centered ambitions and desires to aligning with God's greater plan, I find fulfillment, meaning, and true success.

God encourages me to humbly prioritize serving others and following my purpose, which leads to a more fulfilling and purposeful life, in contrast to the emptiness of ego-driven pursuits. In moments where I feel challenged, I remind myself that my purpose is greater than any temporary emotion. Today, I choose to walk in the power of my purpose, not the emptiness of my ego.

The world is a better place because I am in it.

HEBREWS 13:6 (NIV)

"SO WE CAN CONFIDENTLY SAY, "THE LORD IS MY HELPER; I WILL NOT FEAR; WHAT CAN MAN DO TO ME?"

On my worst days, I matter. On my worst days, my life has meaning. I am a beautiful creation, and when I live with purpose, love, and kindness in my heart, I undoubtedly make the world a brighter and more hopeful place.

I vow to remember that my presence is a gift, and my positive impact on others can impact generations, leaving a lasting legacy of love and inspiration.

My gifts make room for me.

PROVERBS 18:16 (NKJV)

"A MAN'S GIFT MAKES ROOM FOR HIM, AND BRINGS HIM BEFORE GREAT MEN."

I believe that my gift will make room for me. I know that this is a profound testament to the unique talents and abilities that God has blessed me with. My gift is not just a skill; it's a divine tool that can pave the path to my success and purpose. When I nurture and share my gift with the world, I create opportunities for myself and touch the lives of others in meaningful ways.

I trust in the power of my gift, and I know that it has the remarkable ability to open doors I never thought possible, guiding me toward my true calling and making a difference in the lives of the people I encounter.

I leave a powerful legacy of love and service.

MATTHEW 20:28 (NIV)

"JUST AS THE SON OF MAN DID NOT COME TO BE SERVED, BUT TO SERVE, AND TO GIVE HIS LIFE AS A RANSOM FOR MANY."

I know that having a servant's heart is at the core of living a purposeful life. God's Word emphasizes the importance of selflessly serving others. When I give of myself, I contribute to the betterment of the world, just as God called me to.

I make it my mission and life's work to serve with love and compassion. I know this will leave a lasting impact on those I touch. It will also create a powerful legacy of kindness and selflessness. I reflect God's love and light when I serve others, and this legacy of love and service becomes a testament to my faith and the values I hold dear.

My purpose has a global impact.

GENESIS 17:4 (NLT)

"THIS IS MY COVENANT WITH YOU: I WILL MAKE YOU THE FATHER OF A MULTITUDE OF NATIONS."

I accept God's call for my life, understanding that my purpose carries global significance and impact. Embracing the belief that my purpose has a global impact is a divine example of the boundless potential that I possess.

God's Word reaffirms that my purpose extends far beyond my immediate surroundings. By aligning my actions and endeavors with God's plan, I am a beacon of His love, wisdom, and grace to people around the world. As I touch lives, inspire change, and spread positivity, I fulfill my purpose on a global scale, leaving a meaningful and lasting impact for His glory.

I am a living manifestation of my ancestors' wildest dreams.

PSALM 102:18 (ESV)

"LET THIS BE RECORDED FOR A GENERATION TO COME, SO THAT A PEOPLE YET TO BE CREATED MAY PRAISE THE LORD."

I know that I am a living manifestation of my ancestors' wildest dreams, and this fills my heart with gratitude and purpose.

God calls me to honor the legacy of those who came before me. Each step I take, each success I achieve, is a tribute to the dreams and sacrifices of those who paved the way. As I live my life in alignment with God's plan, I become a living testament to the faith, strength, and resilience of my ancestors, carrying their hopes and dreams forward into a brighter future.

I stop wasting my time trying to convince people of my purpose and vision.

GALATIANS 1:10(ESV)

"FOR AM I NOW SEEKING THE APPROVAL OF MAN, OR OF GOD? OR AM I TRYING TO PLEASE MAN? IF I WERE STILL TRYING TO PLEASE MAN, I WOULD NOT BE A SERVANT OF CHRIST."

I understand that my purpose and vision are divine gifts from God, and I find solace in God's promises for my life.

My true calling is to serve God and follow the path He has set for me rather than seeking the validation of others. By focusing my efforts on fulfilling my purpose and trusting in God's plan, I can confidently move forward, knowing that His approval is what truly matters.

I speak only as the Holy Spirit speaks to me.

2 SAMUEL 23:2 (NIV)

"THE SPIRIT OF THE LORD SPEAKS THROUGH ME; HIS WORD IS ON MY TONGUE."

I understand that it is crucial that I align my words with the wisdom of the Holy Spirit. This verse emphasizes the importance of allowing the Holy Spirit to guide my speech, ensuring that my words are filled with wisdom, love, and divine guidance. By speaking as the Holy Spirit leads me, I can bring blessings and inspiration to those around me, fostering a more profound connection with God and others.

I am using my influence to help others.

MATTHEW 5:16 (NIV)

"IN THE SAME WAY, LET YOUR LIGHT SHINE BEFORE OTHERS, THAT THEY MAY SEE YOUR GOOD DEEDS AND GLORIFY YOUR FATHER IN HEAVEN."

My life experiences have taught me the importance of using my influence to positively impact the lives of others. As a believer, I am called to be a beacon of light and love in the world, and one powerful way to do that is by helping and inspiring others through my actions and words.

By using my influence for the betterment of those around me, I not only fulfill my Christian duty but also reflect God's love and grace to the world.

I am shifting to my yes season.

2 CORINTHIANS 9:10 (ESV)

"HE WHO SUPPLIES SEED TO THE SOWER AND BREAD FOR FOOD WILL SUPPLY AND MULTIPLY YOUR SEED FOR SOWING AND INCREASE THE HARVEST OF YOUR RIGHTEOUSNESS."

Life is a series of seasons, and each season serves a purpose in my journey. As I shift into my YES season, I embrace the opportunities and blessings that God has prepared for me. It's a season of alignment with His will, where I step into the fullness of His plan for my life, saying "yes" to His guidance and purpose. This shift brings forth abundant blessings and fulfillment as I walk in faith and trust in His divine timing.

God opens doors for me that no one can close.

REVELATION 3:7 (NIV)

"TO THE ANGEL OF THE CHURCH IN PHILADELPHIA WRITE: THESE ARE THE WORDS OF HIM WHO IS HOLY AND TRUE, WHO HOLDS THE KEY OF DAVID. WHAT HE OPENS, NO ONE CAN SHUT, AND WHAT HE SHUTS, NO ONE CAN OPEN."

When God opens a door in my life, it is a divine portal that no one can hinder or close. His plans and blessings are unstoppable, and as I learn to trust in His guidance and timing, I can move forward with confidence, knowing that His doors of opportunity will lead me to greater fulfillment, blessings, and success. It is time for me to walk through the doors He has opened for me.

I am clear about my purpose.

PROVERBS 19:21 (NIV)

"MANY ARE THE PLANS IN A PERSON'S HEART, BUT IT IS THE LORD'S PURPOSE THAT PREVAILS."

I seek God's purpose for me daily, asking Him to guide me and order my steps. When I align myself with His divine plan, I gain clarity and direction.

Knowing my purpose brings focus, fulfillment, and a sense of calling that guides me in all aspects of life, including my career, relationships, and daily decisions. As I seek His purpose, I can confidently proclaim that I have clarity about my God-given calling, and I am walking in the path He has set before me.

I am going to the next level; I go from faith to faith.

ROMANS 1:17 (NIV)

"FOR IN THE GOSPEL THE RIGHTEOUSNESS OF GOD IS REVEALED—A RIGHTEOUSNESS THAT IS BY FAITH FROM FIRST TO LAST, JUST AS IT IS WRITTEN: 'THE RIGHTEOUS WILL LIVE BY FAITH.'"

This scripture affirms the principle of continuous growth and progress in my faith journey. As I move forward, I do so by faith, trusting that God is leading me to the next level. With unwavering belief, I transition from one level of faith to another, stepping into the blessings and purpose that He has prepared for me. This journey from faith to faith magnifies my faithfulness and trust in God's divine plan for my life.

I take massive action to fulfill my purpose.

JAMES 2:17 (NIV)

"IN THE SAME WAY, FAITH BY ITSELF IF IT IS NOT ACCOMPANIED BY ACTION, IS DEAD."

This scripture emphasizes the importance of acting in alignment with my faith and purpose. It teaches me that faith without corresponding actions cannot bring about the outcomes I desire. By taking massive action in pursuit of my purpose, I honor God's plan for my life and demonstrate my trust in Him. Through my actions, I bring my purpose to life, impacting my life and the lives of those around me, all in accordance with God's divine guidance.

I refuse to dim my light or play small to make others feel comfortable.

EPHESIANS 5:8 (ESV)

"FOR AT ONE TIME, YOU WERE DARKNESS, BUT NOW YOU ARE LIGHT IN THE LORD. WALK AS CHILDREN OF LIGHT."

I am called to shine brightly, dispelling darkness with my inner light. By refusing to dim my light or play small, I boldly and unapologetically honor my divine purpose and the gifts God has given me. It is through my unapologetic authenticity and radiant light that I inspire and uplift others, showing them the way to walk in the light of the Lord as well.

My best years are ahead of me.

PHILIPPIANS 3:13-14 (NIV)

"BROTHERS AND SISTERS, I DO NOT CONSIDER MYSELF YET TO HAVE TAKEN HOLD OF IT. BUT ONE THING I DO: FORGETTING WHAT IS BEHIND AND STRAINING TOWARD WHAT IS AHEAD, I PRESS ON TOWARD THE GOAL TO WIN THE PRIZE FOR WHICH GOD HAS CALLED ME HEAVENWARD IN CHRIST JESUS."

I rejoice in the promises of God, holding steadfast and believing that my best years are indeed ahead of me. I release the burdens of the past, embrace the lessons I've learned, and I look forward with faith and determination. With God's guidance and my commitment, I can press on toward my goals, confident that He has a bright and purposeful future in store for me.

I am not afraid to dream big.

EXODUS 35:31-32 (ESV)

"AND HE HAS FILLED HIM WITH THE SPIRIT OF GOD, WITH SKILL, WITH INTELLIGENCE, WITH KNOWLEDGE, AND WITH ALL CRAFTSMANSHIP, TO DEVISE ARTISTIC DESIGNS, TO WORK IN GOLD AND SILVER AND BRONZE."

God has endowed me with various talents, skills, and intelligence. He has given me the ability to dream big and pursue my passions with creativity and craftsmanship.

When I recognize and embrace these gifts from Him, there is no reason for me to be afraid to dream big. I choose to trust in His guidance and use my abilities to their fullest potential, knowing that God is with me every step of the way, just as He was with those who crafted beautiful works in gold, silver, and bronze in His Word.

I break generational curses.

GALATIANS 5:1 (ESV)

"FOR FREEDOM, CHRIST HAS SET US FREE; STAND FIRM THEREFORE, AND DO NOT SUBMIT AGAIN TO A YOKE OF SLAVERY."

God's Word reminds me that through my faith in Christ, I have the strength to break free from the chains of generational curses. I can choose a different path, one filled with God's grace and blessings. By seeking His guidance and walking in His ways, I break the cycle for myself and future generations, allowing His love and freedom to prevail in my life.

I live an authentic and transparent life.

EPHESIANS 4:25 (ESV)

"THEREFORE, HAVING PUT AWAY FALSEHOOD, LET EACH ONE OF YOU SPEAK THE TRUTH WITH HIS NEIGHBOR, FOR WE ARE MEMBERS ONE OF ANOTHER."

Living an authentic and transparent life reflects the teachings of God's Word. His direction encourages me to be genuine in my interactions with others, to cast aside falsehood, and to embrace honesty and transparency. By doing so, I build trust, foster deeper connections, and create an atmosphere of love and authenticity in my relationships and endeavors.

I embrace and embody my divine inheritance from God.

ROMANS 8:17 (BLB)

"AND IF CHILDREN, ALSO HEIRS: HEIRS INDEED OF GOD, AND JOINT-HEIRS OF CHRIST, IF INDEED WE SUFFER WITH *HIM*, SO THAT WE MAY ALSO BE GLORIFIED TOGETHER."

I embrace and embody my divine inheritance from God as powerful proof of my faith and belief in His promises. The Word of God reminds me that as His child, I inherit His blessings, grace, and eternal love. By embracing this divine inheritance, I tap into my true potential, live with purpose, and carry myself with the confidence that I am loved and supported by the Creator of the universe. This fills me with strength, courage, and inspiration in my journey through life.

I have been created by God to prosper and make a difference in the world.

JEREMIAH 29:11 (NIV)

"FOR I KNOW THE PLANS I HAVE FOR YOU, DECLARES THE LORD, PLANS FOR WELFARE AND NOT FOR EVIL, TO GIVE YOU A FUTURE AND A HOPE."

I am divinely created by God with unique gifts, talents, and a purpose that's meant to prosper and make a positive impact in the world. God has intentional plans for me, plans that lead to prosperity, hope, and a brighter future. By recognizing and embracing this truth, I find the strength and motivation to pursue my dreams, serve others, and leave a legacy of love and purpose.

Let your Life be affirmed

August:
Healing From Past Trauma

Freeing Yourself from the Bondage of Your Past Pain

This month's affirmations delve into the profound journey of healing from past trauma and emerging stronger than ever before. Life often presents us with trials and tribulations that leave us scarred, but as people of faith, we understand that God is our ultimate healer. We explore the importance of facing our pain, acknowledging our wounds, and seeking the divine solace that helps us mend the broken pieces of our hearts.

Through the lens of our faith, we learn that even in our darkest moments, God's light shines upon us, guiding us toward recovery. We discover how to turn our pain into purpose. As we walk this path of healing, we find comfort in the knowledge that we are not alone; God is our ever-present source of strength and restoration.

This month, I encourage you to embrace the power of forgiveness, both for yourself and for those who have caused you harm. Recognize that forgiveness is not a sign of weakness but a testament to your faith and the release of burdens that weigh you down. This month's affirmations explore the beauty of resilience, understanding that your scars are not signs of defeat but badges of honor, showcasing your triumph over adversity. You are not a victim, but a victor in Christ, our redeemer!

At the end of this month, you will emerge as a wounded healer, ready to extend your love and support to others who may be on a similar journey. Through your experiences, you become a beacon of hope, demonstrating that healing is possible, and a brighter future awaits those who dare to rise from the ashes of their past, just as you have.

Through faith, love, and resilience, you will find that even the most broken pieces of your life can be transformed into a beautiful mosaic of God's grace and purpose.

I forgive myself for not knowing better in the past.

PSALM 103:2-3 (ESV)

"BLESS THE LORD, O MY SOUL, AND FORGET NOT ALL HIS BENEFITS, WHO FORGIVES ALL YOUR INIQUITY, WHO HEALS ALL YOUR DISEASES."

Forgiving self for past mistakes and shortcomings is a profound act of self-compassion and faith. It's a recognition that I am imperfect and bound to make errors along the way. When I choose to forgive myself, I open the door to healing, growth, and a brighter future. God's love and grace extend not only to forgiving others but also to forgiving myself. It's a beautiful reminder that our past does not define our future, and through forgiveness, I pave the way for a more loving and abundant life.

I love and accept myself, regardless of my past mistakes.

PSALM 34:18 (ESV)

"THE LORD IS NEAR TO THE BROKENHEARTED AND SAVES THE CRUSHED IN SPIRIT."

I love and accept myself, regardless of my past mistakes. I recognize that this is a profound reflection of God's unconditional love for me. In the eyes of the Creator, I am forgiven, cherished, and worthy of His grace.

When I extend that same love and acceptance to myself, I align with the divine truth that I am fearfully and wonderfully made. My past may include imperfections and errors, but it is also a testimony to my growth, resilience, and capacity for change.

By choosing to love and accept myself, I honor the redemptive power of God's love in my life. This self-compassion enables me to move forward with confidence, embracing the beautiful journey of transformation that God has laid before me.

I release the weight of my past and embrace a future of healing.

PSALM 147:3 (NIV)

"HE HEALS THE BROKENHEARTED AND BINDS UP THEIR WOUNDS."

I release the heavy burdens of my past as a liberating act of faith. I am shedding the weight of old chains that have held me back for far too long. God called me to trust in the promise of healing and redemption through my faith in Him.

When I release the weight of my past, I make space for His divine grace and transformative power to work within me. This allows me to step into a future filled with hope, knowing that my scars do not define me, but rather, they are evidence of my strength and resilience.

By embracing this future of healing, I declare and stand boldly on my trust in God's plan for my life, allowing Him to lead me toward greater purpose and wholeness.

I do not hold on to previous versions of myself because I have evolved.

ISAIAH 41:10 (ESV)

"FEAR NOT, FOR I AM WITH YOU; BE NOT DISMAYED, FOR I AM YOUR GOD; I WILL STRENGTHEN YOU, I WILL HELP YOU, I WILL UPHOLD YOU WITH MY RIGHTEOUS RIGHT HAND."

I know that embracing my personal evolution is a beautiful example of God's work in my life. As a believer, I understand that growth and transformation are essential elements of my faith journey.

Holding onto previous versions of myself can hinder the progress God intends for me. By letting go of who I used to be, I make space for the person God is molding me to be—a vessel of His love, grace, and purpose.

My past may contain lessons, but it does not shackle me. By releasing these old versions of myself, I open the door to becoming more aligned with God's divine plan and fully embracing the path of spiritual and personal growth He has laid before me.

I am not responsible for what other people think about my past.

ISAIAH 53:5 (NIV)

"BUT HE WAS PIERCED FOR OUR TRANSGRESSIONS; HE WAS CRUSHED FOR OUR INIQUITIES; UPON HIM WAS THE CHASTISEMENT THAT BROUGHT US PEACE, AND WITH HIS WOUNDS, WE ARE HEALED."

My identity is rooted in Christ, not in the opinions or judgments of others. I am not accountable for how people perceive my past or the choices I've made. I am called to focus on God's forgiveness and grace, which offer me a daily fresh start and a new identity in Him.

While others may have their own perspectives, I can rest in the assurance that God's love and acceptance of me is unchanging. My past, with all its ups and downs, is part of my journey, but it doesn't define me. My identity is found in being a child of God, redeemed and made new through His love and forgiveness.

I accept God's love and forgiveness.

PSALM 103:2-3 (ESV)

"BLESS THE LORD, O MY SOUL, AND FORGET NOT ALL HIS BENEFITS, WHO FORGIVES ALL YOUR INIQUITY, WHO HEALS ALL YOUR DISEASES."

I am inherently worthy of God's love and forgiveness, and I accept it as a transformative and deeply liberating experience. It allows me to release the burdens of guilt and shame that may have weighed me down in the past.

When I embrace God's boundless love and His gift of forgiveness, I open myself up to a world of healing and renewal. It's a powerful acknowledgment that, despite my imperfections and mistakes, I am unconditionally loved by my Creator.

This acceptance not only strengthens my relationship with God but also empowers me to extend love and forgiveness to myself and others, fostering a greater sense of inner peace and harmony.

I am not defined by my past; I am shaped by my strength.

ROMANS 15:13 (ESV)

"MAY THE GOD OF HOPE FILL YOU WITH ALL JOY AND PEACE IN BELIEVING, SO THAT BY THE POWER OF THE HOLY SPIRIT YOU MAY ABOUND IN HOPE."

My past does not define me. It serves as a backdrop, highlighting the strength of God's grace and mercy, which shines brilliantly in my life. I carry a richly unique story filled with triumphs and trials.

While I cannot change my history, I have the incredible God-given power to manifest and shape my present and future through the strength that I have discovered within myself. My past experiences, both the joyful and the challenging, have equipped me with valuable lessons and a wellspring of inner fortitude.

By embracing this truth, I unlock the power to overcome obstacles, pursue my dreams, and become the best version of myself. I am not limited by my past; I am defined by God's love for me. It is this unconditional love and grace that propels me forward on my journey toward growth and purpose.

Healing is a journey, and I am on the path to wholeness.

JEREMIAH 17:14 (ESV)

"HEAL ME, O LORD, AND I SHALL BE HEALED; SAVE ME, AND I SHALL BE SAVED, FOR YOU ARE MY PRAISE."

My lifelong healing journey leads me through the most profound transformations. It's a path of self-discovery, self-compassion, and self-restoration. As I navigate the winding road of healing, I encounter moments of reflection, forgiveness, and growth.

I know that healing is not a destination but a continuous process, a sacred journey toward wholeness. Along this path, I release the burdens of the past, take responsibility for mending my broken pieces, and embrace the beauty of my scars. I am on this journey, walking hand in hand with the Divine, guided by grace and fueled by faith, knowing that with each step, I inch closer to the profound sense of wholeness that my heart deeply desires.

I forgive my parents for not being who or what I needed them to be.

ISAIAH 43:18-19 (ESV)

"REMEMBER NOT THE FORMER THINGS, NOR CONSIDER THE THINGS OF OLD. BEHOLD, I AM DOING A NEW THING; NOW IT SPRINGS FORTH, DO YOU NOT PERCEIVE IT? I WILL MAKE A WAY IN THE WILDERNESS AND RIVERS IN THE DESERT."

Forgiveness is a powerful act of love and healing, and it liberates not only the people I forgive but also me. My parents may have fallen short of my expectations or needs, but forgiveness is essential for my emotional healing and growth.

As I extend forgiveness to my parents, I release the burdens of resentment and disappointment that can weigh me down. I recognize that they, too, are human and have their own imperfections and struggles.

Through forgiveness, I embrace a sense of peace and freedom, which allows me to move forward with compassion and a renewed perspective on my life's journey. It's an act of grace that leads to personal healing and transformation.

I am surrounded by love and support on my healing journey.

PSALM 55:22 (ESV)

"CAST YOUR BURDEN ON THE LORD, AND HE WILL SUSTAIN YOU; HE WILL NEVER PERMIT THE RIGHTEOUS TO BE MOVED."

God has surrounded me with His love and support along my healing journey. Embracing this love and support is a crucial step toward my wholeness and transformation. I was not meant to walk this path alone; God has placed loving and supportive people in my life to uplift and encourage me.

I am so grateful for my friends, family, mentors, and fellow believers who offer a listening ear, a comforting presence, and prayers on my behalf. Their love and support remind me that I am cherished and valued, regardless of my past or wounds.

With this network of care, I find strength in vulnerability, and together, we create a nurturing environment where healing can take place. It's a beautiful reminder that God's love is manifested through the love and support of those who walk beside me on my journey to wholeness.

My inner strength guides me toward a life of peace and joy.

PSALM 119:105 (ESV)

"YOUR WORD IS A LAMP TO MY FEET AND A LIGHT TO MY PATH."

Inner strength, nurtured by faith and resilience, serves as a steadfast compass guiding me toward a life filled with peace and joy. This inner fortitude empowers me daily to face life's challenges with courage and unwavering determination. It reminds me that, despite the storms that may come my way, I possess the ability to find calm amid chaos and discover joy even in difficult circumstances.

As I cultivate this inner strength through prayer, self-reflection, and a deep connection with God, it becomes the driving force that allows me to embrace each day with gratitude and a heart filled with hope. It is a tribute to the evidentiary power of faith, reminding me that I can live a life that radiates peace and overflows with joy, regardless of external circumstances.

I use the lessons I learned in the past to make a better future for myself.

PSALM 30:5 (ESV)

"FOR HIS ANGER IS BUT FOR A MOMENT, AND HIS FAVOR IS FOR A LIFETIME. WEEPING MAY TARRY FOR THE NIGHT, BUT JOY COMES WITH THE MORNING."

The lessons from my past are not burdens to carry but valuable tools to forge a brighter future. Each experience, whether joyful or challenging, serves as a steppingstone towards personal growth and a better future.

I have the power to extract wisdom from my past choices and circumstances, using them as building blocks for a more purposeful and fulfilling life. It's through these lessons that I discover resilience, determination, and the capacity to create a future that aligns with my God-given purpose. By applying the knowledge gleaned from my past, I can navigate life's journey with wisdom, grace, and a deep sense of hope, knowing that each step forward is an opportunity to make my future even brighter.

I am capable of transforming pain into purpose.

ISAIAH 61:3 (ESV)

"TO GRANT TO THOSE WHO MOURN IN ZION— TO GIVE THEM A BEAUTIFUL HEADDRESS INSTEAD OF ASHES, THE OIL OF GLADNESS INSTEAD OF MOURNING, THE GARMENT OF PRAISE INSTEAD OF A FAINT SPIRIT; THAT THEY MAY BE CALLED OAKS OF RIGHTEOUSNESS, THE PLANTING OF THE LORD, THAT HE MAY BE GLORIFIED."

As a believer, I am empowered by the grace and love of God to transform my pain into purpose. Even during life's most challenging moments, I can find the strength to rise above my circumstances and use my experiences as catalysts for positive change.

It is through these trials that I discover my resilience, compassion, and capacity to make a meaningful impact on the world. When I surrender my pain to God, He can guide me toward a purpose that not only heals my wounds but also brings healing and hope to others. My past pain becomes a testimony of God's redemptive power, reminding me that, with His grace, I am more than a conqueror.

I am not broken; I am a work in progress.

JEREMIAH 30:17 (ESV)

"FOR I WILL RESTORE HEALTH TO YOU, AND YOUR WOUNDS I WILL HEAL, DECLARES THE LORD."

When God looks at me, He does not see brokenness. He sees an unfinished, yet splendidly beautiful, masterpiece. I am a beautiful work in progress, continuously being molded and refined by the hands of the Divine Potter.

My imperfections are not signs of failure but opportunities for growth and transformation. As I journey through life, I consciously embrace the truth that I am a masterpiece in the making, crafted with love and purpose. Each day provides me with a chance to become more aligned with the image God has of me. Today, I release self-condemnation and self-doubt, for I am not broken; I am a masterpiece in progress and walking proof of God's grace and endless love.

I deserve to live a life free from the grip of past trauma.

PSALM 30:2 (ESV)

"O LORD MY GOD, I CRIED TO YOU FOR HELP, AND YOU HAVE HEALED ME."

I deserve to live a life unburdened by the shadows of past trauma. As a child of the King, this is my divine birthright. My Creator wants me to experience His boundless love, grace, and peace. He doesn't intend for me to carry the weight of my past like an anchor, holding me back from the abundant life He has in store for me.

I am worthy of healing, of rediscovering my joy, and of stepping into a future where my past no longer defines me. Through faith, support, and self-compassion, I can break free from the chains of trauma and embrace the fullness of life that God has prepared for me. My journey to healing is evidence of my strength and resilience. I absolutely deserve to live a life filled with hope and freedom.

I am stronger than I ever imagined, and I continue to grow.

2 TIMOTHY 1:7 (ESV)

"FOR GOD GAVE US A SPIRIT NOT OF FEAR BUT OF POWER, LOVE, AND SELF-CONTROL."

My strength and my capacity for growth in Christ Jesus knows no bounds. With faith as my foundation, I have tapped into a fountain of resilience and inner fortitude. Every challenge I have faced, every obstacle I have overcome, has contributed to my remarkable strength. But it doesn't stop there – I am continually evolving, growing, and becoming an even better version of myself.

God's grace empowers me to rise above circumstances and embrace my true potential. I possess a strength that defies expectations, and my journey is a testament to the boundless possibilities that lie ahead. I embrace my strength, I will keep growing, and I will let it illuminate the path to a life filled with purpose and fulfillment.

Each day brings me closer to complete healing and restoration.

PHILIPPIANS 4:6-7 (ESV)

"DO NOT BE ANXIOUS ABOUT ANYTHING, BUT IN EVERYTHING BY PRAYER AND SUPPLICATION WITH THANKSGIVING LET YOUR REQUESTS BE MADE KNOWN TO GOD. AND THE PEACE OF GOD, WHICH SURPASSES ALL UNDERSTANDING, WILL GUARD YOUR HEARTS AND YOUR MINDS IN CHRIST JESUS."

Each day is a step forward on my journey towards complete healing and restoration. With each sunrise, God graces me with the opportunity to mend, to grow, and to flourish. I carry within me the resilience and determination to overcome any obstacle in my path. My faith is the driving force that guides me through the healing process, renewing my spirit and filling my heart with hope.

As I continue to walk in God's light, I draw nearer to a state of wholeness, where my scars become badges of honor, and my past wounds are transformed into my greatest sources of strength.

Each new day is a testament to my unwavering commitment to healing, and it brings me one step closer to the beautiful restoration that God has in store for my life.

I release shame and guilt, embracing self-compassion.

PSALM 42:11 (ESV)

"WHY ARE YOU CAST DOWN, O MY SOUL, AND WHY ARE YOU IN TURMOIL WITHIN ME? HOPE IN GOD; FOR I SHALL AGAIN PRAISE HIM, MY SALVATION, AND MY GOD."

In the loving embrace of God's grace, I have found the strength to release the heavy burdens of shame and guilt that once weighed me down. I've come to understand that these emotions serve no purpose in my journey toward healing and self-discovery.

Instead, I choose to envelop myself in the warm and comforting blanket of self-compassion. God's love has taught me that I am worthy of forgiveness, and by extending that forgiveness to myself, I open my heart to healing. With each act of self-compassion, I create space for my growth, joy, and a renewed sense of purpose. I am no longer defined by my past mistakes; I am defined by the boundless love and compassion I offer to myself and others.

I give myself grace while I am healing and transitioning.

LAMENTATIONS 3:22-23 (ESV)

"THE STEADFAST LOVE OF THE LORD NEVER CEASES; HIS MERCIES NEVER COME TO AN END; THEY ARE NEW EVERY MORNING; GREAT IS YOUR FAITHFULNESS."

As I walk the path of healing and transition, I've learned the beautiful art of giving myself grace. Just as God showers His unending grace upon me every day, I've come to realize that extending that same grace to myself is a profound act of self-love.

I understand that healing takes time and that transitions can be challenging, but in these moments of growth and transformation, I choose to be gentle with myself. I acknowledge that it's okay to have moments of vulnerability, doubt, or even temporary setbacks.

Through it all, I hold myself in a compassionate embrace, allowing myself the space to heal at my own pace. This grace I offer myself is a tribute to my faith, strength, and resilience, and it paves the way for a brighter, more empowered future.

I am resilient, and I can bounce back from anything life throws at me.

PSALM 107:20 (ESV)

"HE SENT OUT HIS WORD AND HEALED THEM AND DELIVERED THEM FROM THEIR DESTRUCTION."

I am a testament to the incredible resilience that dwells within me. Life's challenges may have knocked me down at times, but because of God's love and grace, they have never kept me down. With unwavering faith and determination, I rise stronger each time, bouncing back from adversity with a renewed spirit.

I understand that setbacks are not the end of my story but rather opportunities for growth and transformation. My resilience is like a mighty oak tree, firmly rooted in faith and nourished by the living waters of hope. I believe in my ability to overcome, and this unshakeable faith is a beacon of inspiration to those who hear my empowering message.

My life is a living testament to the limitless strength that comes from a deep connection with God. I walk with the confidence of a resilient overcomer, ready to face any challenge that comes my way.

I hold space for my loved ones as they heal.

JAMES 5:16 (ESV)

"THEREFORE, CONFESS YOUR SINS TO ONE ANOTHER AND PRAY FOR ONE ANOTHER, THAT YOU MAY BE HEALED. THE PRAYER OF A RIGHTEOUS PERSON HAS GREAT POWER AS IT IS WORKING."

I have a compassionate heart that embraces my loved ones with unwavering support and understanding as they embark on their own healing journeys. I lovingly create a safe and nurturing space where they can freely express their pain, fears, and hopes.

My presence is a comforting refuge, a haven of solace where they can release their burdens and find solace in the midst of life's storms. I know the profound value of being there for the people I love as they heal. I offer a listening ear, a caring shoulder, and an empathetic soul.

My love and support play a vital role in the healing process of my loved ones. I encourage and uplift them as they move toward wholeness, reminding them that they are never alone on their path to restoration. My love and support shine as a beacon of hope and healing for the people closest to me.

I choose healing over suffering, love over fear, and growth over stagnation.

PROVERBS 3:5-6 (ESV)

"TRUST IN THE LORD WITH ALL YOUR HEART, AND DO NOT LEAN ON YOUR UNDERSTANDING. IN ALL YOUR WAYS ACKNOWLEDGE HIM, AND HE WILL MAKE STRAIGHT YOUR PATHS."

I am a beacon of light and a testament to the power of choice. Every day, I make the conscious decision to prioritize my own healing journey, embracing the transformative forces of love and growth. Instead of allowing suffering to define my path, I rise above it, determined to find strength in vulnerability and courage in the face of fear.

My unwavering commitment to healing not only transforms my own life but serves as an inspiring example to others. I understand that choosing healing is not a one-time decision but a daily commitment, and I walk this path with grace and determination. By consistently choosing love, growth, and healing, I radiate positivity and inspire those around me to do the same, creating a ripple effect of transformation and renewal.

I choose to forgive and let go, freeing myself from the chains of trauma.

ISAIAH 40:31 (ESV)

"BUT THEY WHO WAIT FOR THE LORD SHALL RENEW THEIR STRENGTH; THEY SHALL MOUNT UP WITH WINGS LIKE EAGLES; THEY SHALL RUN AND NOT BE WEARY; THEY SHALL WALK AND NOT FAINT."

Forgiveness is the key that unlocks the shackles of my past, and I wield it with grace and strength. I have made the powerful choice to release the burdens of trauma and pain, recognizing that holding onto them only hinders my growth and happiness.

As I extend forgiveness to others and, most importantly, to myself, I experience a profound sense of liberation. With each act of forgiveness, I break the chains that have bound me, allowing my spirit to soar freely. This choice is not a sign of weakness but a testament to my inner strength and resilience. By embracing forgiveness, I pave the way for a brighter, more peaceful future, unburdened by the weight of the past.

I find healthy and productive ways to cope when I feel triggered.

1 PETER 5:7 (ESV)

"CASTING ALL YOUR ANXIETIES ON HIM BECAUSE HE CARES FOR YOU."

In moments of vulnerability and emotional turbulence, I demonstrate remarkable resilience by choosing healthy and productive coping strategies. Rather than succumbing to the turmoil, I draw upon my inner strength and the wisdom of my faith to navigate these challenges.

Through prayer, mindfulness, and seeking support from loved ones and my community, I have learned to transform triggering moments into opportunities for growth and self-discovery. This practice not only empowers me but also serves as an inspiring example to those around me.

By choosing these constructive pathways, I am actively shaping a life of emotional wellness and encouraging others to do the same.

My past trauma did not happen to me, it happened for me.

ROMANS 8:28 (NIV)

"AND WE KNOW THAT IN ALL THINGS GOD WORKS FOR THE GOOD OF THOSE WHO LOVE HIM, WHO HAVE BEEN CALLED ACCORDING TO HIS PURPOSE."

I have a profound perspective on my past trauma, recognizing that it wasn't merely an event that happened to me but a significant part of my journey designed to lead me to greater purpose and healing.

My faith has provided me with the strength and insight to see the silver lining in the most challenging moments of my life. By embracing this perspective, I transform my pain into a powerful source of motivation and empathy. I understand that these experiences have equipped me with unique insights and compassion, allowing me to connect with others who may be going through similar challenges.

My journey proves the transformative power of faith and resilience, and it inspires those around me to view their own traumas as stepping-stones toward a brighter future.

I release negative emotions and make room for healing.

MARK 5:34 (ESV)

"AND HE SAID TO HER, 'DAUGHTER, YOUR FAITH HAS MADE YOU WELL; GO IN PEACE AND BE HEALED OF YOUR DISEASE.'"

I possess the wisdom to recognize the importance of releasing negative emotions as a crucial step toward healing. My faith and mindset guide me in letting go of the burdens that weigh down my spirit.

By releasing these negative emotions, I create a spacious and fertile ground within my heart, ready to receive the seeds of hope, joy, and restoration. I understand that holding onto negativity only hinders my growth and prevents me from fully embracing the blessings and opportunities that God has in store for me.

Through prayer, self-reflection, and a commitment to positivity, I continually make room for healing, allowing God's love and grace to flow freely into my life.

I am better today than I was yesterday; I celebrate the progress that I have made.

PSALM 51:10 (ESV)

"CREATE IN ME A CLEAN HEART, O GOD, AND RENEW A RIGHT SPIRIT WITHIN ME."

Every step I take, no matter how small it may seem, is evidence of God's enduring strength and love. These divine gifts fuel me with resilience and determination. Instead of dwelling on my past shortcomings, I choose to focus on my growth and the positive changes I've embraced.

This attitude of celebration and gratitude not only bolsters my self-esteem but also serves as a source of inspiration for those who look up to me. With God's guidance, I continue to evolve into the best version of myself, cherishing each day's progress as a valuable gift on my journey to becoming the person He designed me to be.

My body, mind, and spirit are aligned for optimal healing.

2 CORINTHIANS 1:3-4 (ESV)

"BLESSED BE THE GOD AND FATHER OF OUR LORD JESUS CHRIST, THE FATHER OF MERCIES AND GOD OF ALL COMFORT, WHO COMFORTS US IN ALL OUR AFFLICTION, SO THAT WE MAY BE ABLE TO COMFORT THOSE WHO ARE IN ANY AFFLICTION, WITH THE COMFORT WITH WHICH WE OURSELVES ARE COMFORTED BY GOD."

I am in tune with the incredible power of alignment. My body, mind, and spirit are working harmoniously toward optimal healing. By acknowledging this alignment, I open myself to the fullness of God's healing grace. My body, as His temple, is a vessel for His divine healing energy.

My mind, when filled with faith and positive thoughts, becomes a powerful tool for transformation. And my spirit, connected to the source of all healing, is a wellspring of strength and resilience.

I understand that true healing encompasses not only physical well-being but also emotional and spiritual wholeness. In this alignment, I find the path to complete restoration, ready to embrace each day with renewed vitality and purpose.

I am worthy of happiness, and I am healing to achieve it.

PSALM 107:19-20 (NIV)

"THEN THEY CRIED TO THE LORD IN THEIR TROUBLE, AND HE DELIVERED THEM FROM THEIR DISTRESS. HE SENT OUT HIS WORD AND HEALED THEM AND DELIVERED THEM FROM THEIR DESTRUCTION."

I am worthy of happiness, and I am actively pursuing it through my healing journey. In the eyes of my Creator, I am His beloved child, and my worthiness is beyond measure.

My path to healing shows my strength and resilience, and it is leading me toward a life filled with happiness, peace, and purpose. I embrace the truth that my healing journey is a powerful affirmation of my inherent worthiness.

I am taking the necessary steps to heal, grow, and transform, and as I do, I am drawing closer to the abundant happiness that is destined for me.

I look forward to my future with joy, hope, and optimism.

PSALM 130:5 (NASB1995)

"I WAIT FOR THE LORD, MY SOUL DOES WAIT, AND IN HIS WORD DO I HOPE."

As I continue my journey of healing and personal growth, I look forward to my future with an abundance of joy, hope, and optimism. My faith in God's plan for my life and my commitment to embracing each day with a positive outlook will pave the way for a future filled with blessings and purpose.

I know that my past does not define me; it has shaped me into the strong and resilient person I am today. With each step I take towards healing and with God's guidance, my future will shine even brighter. I embrace the joy that comes from knowing that the best is yet to come, and my hopeful outlook attracts opportunities and blessings beyond my imagination.

I trust in the process of healing, knowing that I am moving forward each day.

ROMANS 12:2 (ESV)

"DO NOT BE CONFORMED TO THIS WORLD, BUT BE TRANSFORMED BY THE RENEWAL OF YOUR MIND, THAT BY TESTING YOU MAY DISCERN WHAT IS THE WILL OF GOD, WHAT IS GOOD AND ACCEPTABLE AND PERFECT."

Trusting the process of healing is a powerful stance to take on my journey. Every day, I commit to healing and taking meaningful steps forward. Just like a seed planted in fertile soil, my healing is a process of growth, transformation, and renewal.

I have faith that with each passing day, I am moving closer to wholeness, restoration, and the abundant life that God has planned for me. I embrace the progress I make, no matter how small it may seem, for it is a testament to my strength and resilience.

I trust in God's timing, and I trust that my healing journey is leading me to a place of peace, joy, and fulfillment.

Let your Life be affirmed

September:

In His Presence

Unlocking The Power of Cultivating Your Relationship with God

This month, we delve into the transformative power of intentional connection with God. It's about recognizing that, more than anything else, God desires a deep and intimate relationship with each of us. When we intentionally seek His presence through prayer, meditation on His Word, and quiet moments of reflection, we open ourselves up to His divine guidance and revelation.

This month is all about the importance of setting aside dedicated time for God, allowing His wisdom and love to permeate our lives. As we draw nearer to Him, we discover that He's been waiting to know us, speak to us, and reveal the profound truths of His Word in ways that profoundly impact our journey of faith.

I prioritize my relationship with God above everything else.

PSALM 42:1 (ESV)

"AS A DEER PANTS FOR FLOWING STREAMS OF WATER, SO PANTS MY SOUL FOR YOU, O GOD."

I prioritize my relationship with God as a testament to my wisdom and understanding of life's true source of strength and guidance. Just as a tree's roots anchor it firmly in the ground, my connection with God roots me in faith, love, and divine purpose.

It is in my relationship with God that I find unwavering support, boundless love, and the wisdom to navigate life's challenges. By keeping God at the center of my existence, I am aligning myself with the Creator of all things, drawing upon His infinite wisdom and grace to lead me through each day. As I prioritize this sacred connection, I discover that it is the cornerstone of my strength, peace, and the wellspring of my inspiration to live a life of purpose and significance.

Spending time with God is my sacred daily ritual.

PSALM 63:1 (NLT)

"O GOD, YOU ARE MY GOD; I EARNESTLY SEARCH FOR YOU. MY SOUL THIRSTS FOR YOU; MY WHOLE BODY LONGS FOR YOU IN THIS PARCHED AND WEARY LAND WHERE THERE IS NO WATER.."

I spend time with God as a sacred daily ritual, as a powerful affirmation of my faith and devotion. In a world filled with distractions and busyness, this intentional act of drawing near to the Divine represents my commitment to living a life of purpose and alignment with God's will.

Each moment I set aside to commune with the Creator is a precious gift to myself, a chance to center my heart and mind, and a reminder that I am not alone on my journey.

In the stillness of these sacred moments, I find solace, guidance, and the strength to face whatever challenges may come my way. This daily ritual deepens my relationship with God and serves as a foundation upon which I build a life of faith, love, and unwavering hope.

I carve out intentional moments to connect with the divine.

JAMES 4:8 (NIV)

"COME NEAR TO GOD AND HE WILL COME NEAR TO YOU. WASH YOUR HANDS, YOU SINNERS, AND PURIFY YOUR HEARTS, YOU DOUBLE MINDED."

Carving out intentional moments to connect with the divine is a beautiful testament to my spiritual journey. During my fast-paced living, it's a reminder that I am a physical and spiritual being, seeking a deeper connection with my Creator.

These moments of intentionality reflect my commitment to nourishing my soul and cultivating a meaningful relationship with God. They are like precious gems scattered throughout my day, where I pause, breathe, and open my heart to divine guidance, wisdom, and grace.

In these sacred moments, I find solace, purpose, and the strength to navigate life's challenges with faith and resilience. My intentional connection with the divine is a source of inspiration, grounding, and unwavering hope, enriching my life in countless ways.

My soul yearns for a deeper connection with God.

JEREMIAH 29:13 (NIV)

"YOU WILL SEEK ME AND FIND ME WHEN YOU SEEK ME WITH ALL YOUR HEART."

My soul's yearning for a deeper connection with God is a witness to the profound spiritual hunger within me. It's a beautiful longing, a divine invitation to explore the depths of my faith and relationship with the Creator.

This yearning is a compass guiding me toward the source of unconditional love, wisdom, and purpose. It's a reminder that amid life's busyness, there's a sacred space within my heart that craves communion with the Divine.

Embracing this yearning, I embark on a journey of spiritual discovery, seeking solace, guidance, and transformation. It's a path of awe and wonder, where I find that the more I seek God, the more I discover the boundless love and grace that await me.

My soul's yearning is a sacred call to a deeper, more fulfilling connection with The One who created me and knows my heart intimately.

In God's presence, I discover the best version of myself.

MATTHEW 6:33 (NIV)

"BUT SEEK FIRST HIS KINGDOM AND HIS RIGHTEOUSNESS, AND ALL THESE THINGS WILL BE GIVEN TO YOU AS WELL.

In the presence of the Almighty, I am truly unveiled and transformed into the best version of myself. It is within those sacred moments of connection, when I draw near to God, that I find the strength to overcome challenges, the wisdom to make sound decisions, and the grace to extend love and compassion to others.

In His presence, I ponder my purpose and the unique gifts He has bestowed upon me. It is there that I discover the depth of His love and the boundless possibilities that lie ahead. Through this divine connection, I am empowered to live a life of purpose, impact, and unwavering faith, becoming a reflection of His divine light in this world.

Each moment with God is a step toward my higher purpose.

PSALM 119:10 (NIV)

"I SEEK YOU WITH ALL MY HEART; DO NOT LET ME STRAY FROM YOUR COMMANDS."

Each moment I spend with God is a cherished step along the path to my higher purpose. In those divine encounters, I find clarity, guidance, and an overwhelming sense of His love and grace.

These moments are intentional, sacred connections that fuel my journey toward fulfilling the purpose He has designed specifically for me. As I draw near to Him, I remember that He has a grand plan for my life, one that transcends my understanding and spans eternity.

With each moment in His presence, I am molded, shaped, and prepared to walk boldly in the direction of my higher purpose, knowing that He is by my side every step of the way.

I create sacred space for communion with the Divine.

HEBREWS 4:16 (NIV)

"LET US THEN APPROACH GOD'S THRONE OF GRACE WITH CONFIDENCE, SO THAT WE MAY RECEIVE MERCY AND FIND GRACE TO HELP US IN OUR TIME OF NEED."

I create a sacred space in my life, a personal sanctuary for deep communion with the Divine. Within this sacred haven, I set aside the distractions of the world, turning my attention to the presence of God. It's a space where I can pour out my heart, share my joys and sorrows, and listen for His gentle voice. In this sacred communion, I find solace, strength, and the profound realization that I am never alone. It's within this space that I discover the true essence of my being and receive divine guidance to navigate life's intricate tapestry.

Every moment spent in this sacred communion enriches my soul and aligns me with God's purpose for my life, reminding me that His presence is my greatest treasure.

My heart is open to receive God's guidance and wisdom.

PSALM 105:4 (NIV)

"LOOK TO THE LORD AND HIS STRENGTH; SEEK HIS FACE ALWAYS."

My heart is a receptive vessel, wide open to receive the boundless guidance and wisdom that God graciously bestows. I stand in awe of His infinite knowledge and understanding, knowing that His divine counsel is the compass that directs my path.

As I seek His wisdom, I am humbled by His willingness to pour His insights into my heart, illuminating the darkest corners of my life. With each passing day, my heart becomes a well of His divine knowledge, and I am forever grateful for the profound transformation it brings.

With an open heart, I embrace the guidance and wisdom of the Almighty, knowing that His light will always lead me on the path of righteousness and purpose.

My life is transformed by the power of divine connection.

PSALM 34:4 (NIV)

"I SOUGHT THE LORD, AND HE ANSWERED ME; HE DELIVERED ME FROM ALL MY FEARS."

The transformative power of divine connection consistently manifests in my life. Through my faith and steadfast belief in God's presence, I have witnessed miracles unfold, obstacles crumble, and blessings pour forth. It is in my deep connection with the Divine that I find strength, purpose, and unshakeable hope.

God's guiding hand has navigated me through the storms of life, revealing opportunities for growth and blessings beyond measure. My life is a beautiful tapestry woven with the threads of divine connection, and I am eternally grateful for the grace that continues to transform my existence.

I honor the sanctity of spending time with God.

PSALM 119:147 (ESV)

"I RISE BEFORE DAWN AND CRY FOR HELP; I HOPE IN YOUR WORDS."

I honor the sanctity of spending time with God. Each moment I set aside for communion with the Divine is a sacred act of devotion and reverence. In those precious moments of connection, His love, grace, and infinite wisdom surround me.

It is in His presence that I find solace, guidance, and the strength to face life's challenges with faith and courage. I cherish these divine encounters, knowing that they shape me into the person I am meant to be.

As I honor the sanctity of these moments, I am filled with profound gratitude for the privilege of deepening my relationship with God, who continually guides and uplifts my soul.

My spiritual growth is my top priority.

ISAIAH 55:6 (NIV)

"SEEK THE LORD WHILE HE MAY BE FOUND; CALL ON HIM WHILE HE IS NEAR."

My spiritual growth is my top priority. I recognize that nurturing my relationship with God and deepening my faith is the cornerstone of a purposeful and fulfilling life. Each day, I dedicate time and energy to seeking His presence, understanding, and wisdom.

Through prayer, meditation, and studying His Word, I am continuously aligning my heart and mind with His divine plan. This commitment to spiritual growth empowers me to navigate life's challenges with grace, love unconditionally, and live in alignment with my God-given purpose.

As I make my spiritual journey a top priority, I open myself to the transformative power of His guidance and embrace the profound blessings that come from walking closely with Him.

I surrender to God's will and find true strength in it.

PROVERBS 8:17 (NIV)

"I LOVE THOSE WHO LOVE ME, AND THOSE WHO SEEK ME FIND ME."

I surrender to God's will and find true strength in it. In letting go of my own desires and aligning my life with His divine purpose, I discover a profound sense of peace and empowerment. Through surrender, I release the burden of trying to control every aspect of my journey, and I trust that God's plan for me is far greater than I can imagine.

In this surrender, I find strength, resilience, and unwavering faith. His will becomes my guiding light, illuminating the path toward a life filled with purpose, love, and blessings.

As I surrender daily, I tap into the true strength that comes from my reliance on Him, and His grace is more than sufficient to carry me through any challenge I may face.

In stillness, I hear God's whispers of wisdom and love.

PSALM 34:19 (NIV)

"THE RIGHTEOUS PERSON MAY HAVE MANY TROUBLES, BUT THE LORD DELIVERS HIM FROM THEM ALL."

In stillness, I hear God's whispers of wisdom and love. Amidst the chaos of life, I intentionally carve out moments of quiet and reflection, knowing that it is in the hushed moments of my heart that I am most attuned to His gentle guidance.

As I quiet my mind and open my spirit, His voice becomes clear and comforting. His wisdom illuminates the path before me, and His love surrounds me like a warm embrace. In the stillness, I find solace, clarity, and a profound sense of connection with my Creator.

It is in these quiet moments, when I am alone with the Creator that I bask in His infinite grace and the boundless depths of His love for me, and I am strengthened.

I trust that time with God aligns me with my purpose.

PSALM 27:8 (NIV)

"MY HEART SAYS OF YOU, 'SEEK HIS FACE!' YOUR FACE, LORD, I WILL SEEK."

I trust that time with God aligns me with my purpose. In the moments when I seek His presence and guidance, my life as a divine design comes to the forefront of my mind. God's wisdom and direction flow into my heart as I spend intentional moments in His company.

Through this sacred connection, I am continually realigned with my true purpose, gaining clarity on the path He has set before me. I trust that as I walk in faith and spend time with my Creator, every step I take is purposeful and in accordance with His plan.

Each moment spent in His presence strengthens my resolve and deepens my understanding of the unique calling He has placed on my life.

My relationship with God is the cornerstone of my life.

EXODUS 33:14 (NIV)

"THE LORD REPLIED, 'MY PRESENCE WILL GO WITH YOU, AND I WILL GIVE YOU REST.'"

My relationship with God is the cornerstone of my life. It's the foundation upon which I build everything else. As I nurture this sacred connection, I find strength, purpose, and support. In the moments of stillness and reflection, I draw closer to the Creator, deepening my understanding of His love and wisdom.

This relationship guides my path, illuminates my purpose, and provides a steadfast source of hope and inspiration. It is the wellspring of resilience and the driving force behind my journey towards becoming the best version of myself.

I am eternally grateful for this unbreakable bond, for in God's presence, I find my truest self and my greatest source of strength.

I am filled with gratitude for the moments I spend with God.

PSALM 119:18 (NIV)

"OPEN MY EYES THAT I MAY SEE WONDERFUL THINGS IN YOUR LAW."

I am filled with gratitude for the moments I spend with God. Each moment of connection with the Divine is a precious gift, a sacred opportunity to draw closer to the source of all love and wisdom. In these moments, I embrace the boundless grace and unwavering support that surrounds me. I am humbled by the depth of God's love and the guidance He provides on my journey.

Gratitude fills my heart for the countless blessings in my life. Through these moments of communion, I find strength, purpose, and a beautifully soothing sense of peace.

Each moment with God is a treasure, a reminder of His infinite goodness, and a wellspring of inspiration to live a life aligned with His divine plan.

My faith deepens as I invest in my relationship with God.

PSALM 119:105 (NIV)

"YOUR WORD IS A LAMP FOR MY FEET, A LIGHT ON MY PATH."

My faith deepens as I invest in my relationship with God. It's a profound journey of growth, discovery, and genuine trust. With each passing day, the love and grace that God bestows upon me overtakes me.

As I invest time, energy, and devotion in nurturing this sacred connection, my faith becomes a grounding force and foundation for every aspect of my life. Through prayer, scripture, and moments of quiet reflection, I find myself drawing closer to God's heart, and in doing so, I experience a profound transformation.

My faith is not just a set of beliefs; it's a living, breathing force that empowers me, guides me, and fills my life with purpose.

I approach God with reverence, knowing the impact on my life.

JOHN 15:7 (NIV)

"IF YOU REMAIN IN ME AND MY WORDS REMAIN IN YOU, ASK WHATEVER YOU WISH, AND IT WILL BE DONE FOR YOU."

Every encounter with the Divine is a sacred moment, a chance to draw near to the source of all wisdom, love, and strength. These reverent moments remind me of the incredible privilege it is to connect with the Creator of the universe.

With a heart full of gratitude, I seek His guidance, His presence, and His blessings. I understand that these moments of reverence are not just rituals; they are transformative experiences that shape my character, renew my spirit, and illuminate my path.

In His presence, I find the clarity, purpose, and deep spiritual fulfillment that guides me in every aspect of my life's journey.

In God's presence, I am renewed and refreshed.

JOHN 4:24 (NIV)

"GOD IS SPIRIT, AND HIS WORSHIPERS MUST WORSHIP IN THE SPIRIT AND IN TRUTH."

In God's presence, I am renewed and refreshed. In God's presence, I find solace, strength, and a profound sense of peace. As I open my heart and soul to His presence, I feel the burdens of life being lifted and the weariness of the world melting away.

It's in His loving embrace that I move in my purpose, my worth, and the boundless possibilities that lie ahead. In His presence, I find the inspiration to persevere, the courage to overcome, and the unwavering faith that fuels my journey.

These sacred moments of renewal are not just a part of my life; they are the very essence of it, guiding me, sustaining me, and transforming me into the person I was created to be.

My soul craves the nourishment of divine connection.

PSALM 16:11 (NIV)

"YOU MAKE KNOWN TO ME THE PATH OF LIFE; YOU WILL FILL ME WITH JOY IN YOUR PRESENCE, WITH ETERNAL PLEASURES AT YOUR RIGHT HAND."

It's an innate longing, an insatiable hunger for the spiritual sustenance that only God can provide. In those moments of communion, my soul finds solace, purpose, and the deep fulfillment it yearns for. It's as if every fiber of my being rejoices in the presence of the divine, knowing that here, I am truly alive.

This connection feeds my spirit, guiding me along life's path with unwavering love and wisdom. It's a hunger that can only be satisfied by drawing closer to the source of all life, and in doing so, my soul's deepest cravings are satiated, and my heart's desires are fulfilled.

I am intentional in seeking God's presence daily.

HEBREWS 10:22 (NIV)

"LET US DRAW NEAR TO GOD WITH A SINCERE HEART AND WITH THE FULL ASSURANCE THAT FAITH BRINGS, HAVING OUR HEARTS SPRINKLED TO CLEANSE US FROM A GUILTY CONSCIENCE AND HAVING OUR BODIES WASHED WITH PURE WATER."

Each morning, I awake with the purpose of drawing nearer to Him, knowing that in His presence, I find guidance, strength, and the unwavering love that sustains me. With every moment I set aside for prayer and reflection, I am deliberate in opening my heart to His divine influence. The incredible privilege it is to commune with the Creator of the universe is found when I seek His presence.

It is in these intentional moments that I discover the true essence of my faith and the deep reservoirs of peace that flow from a relationship with my Heavenly Father.

God's love empowers me to become my best self.

MATTHEW 11:28-29 (NIV)

"COME TO ME, ALL YOU WHO ARE WEARY AND BURDENED, AND I WILL GIVE YOU REST. TAKE MY YOKE UPON YOU AND LEARN FROM ME, FOR I AM GENTLE AND HUMBLE IN HEART, AND YOU WILL FIND REST FOR YOUR SOULS."

God's love is my everything. It is the air I breathe and my saving grace. His love is the foundation upon which I build my life and the driving force behind my personal growth and transformation. Knowing that the Creator of all things loves me unconditionally fills me with confidence and courage.

I am continually inspired to embrace my full potential, knowing that God's love knows no bounds and His grace is more than sufficient. With this divine empowerment, I can face any challenge, overcome any obstacle, and step into the best version of myself, fulfilling the purpose He has set before me with unwavering faith and strength.

My spiritual practice is the compass of my life's journey.

PSALM 51:10 (NIV)

"CREATE IN ME A PURE HEART, O GOD, AND RENEW A STEADFAST SPIRIT WITHIN ME."

It guides me through the twists and turns, the highs and lows, helping me stay centered and aligned with my purpose. Just as a compass points true north, my spiritual practice points me toward God, the source of all wisdom and love. It's in the stillness of prayer, the depth of meditation, and the study of His Word that I find direction, clarity, and inner peace.

This practice is not just a routine; it's a sacred ritual that keeps me grounded and connected to my faith and strengthens my relationship with the divine.

It reminds me that no matter where life's path may lead, I am never alone, and my journey is guided by a higher purpose.

I cherish the moments spent in God's loving embrace.

PSALM 23:1-3 (NIV)

"A PSALM OF DAVID. THE LORD IS MY SHEPHERD, I LACK NOTHING. HE MAKES ME LIE DOWN IN GREEN PASTURES, HE LEADS ME BESIDE QUIET WATERS, HE REFRESHES MY SOUL."

I cherish the moments spent in God's loving embrace. In those precious moments of connection and communion, I find solace, strength, and an overwhelming sense of His boundless love. It's in the stillness of His presence that my soul is refreshed, my spirit renewed, and my heart filled with gratitude.

These moments are like a warm, comforting hug from the Creator, reminding me of His unwavering support and guidance. I bask in His love. I am never alone. His love is the foundation of my faith, the source of my hope, and the fountain of my joy.

My soul is awakened and enriched through prayer and meditation.

1 CHRONICLES 16:11 (NIV)

"LOOK TO THE LORD AND HIS STRENGTH; SEEK HIS FACE ALWAYS."

In those sacred moments of communion with the Divine, I discover a profound sense of purpose and inner peace. Prayer becomes the language of my heart, a direct line to God's wisdom and guidance. Through meditation, I find stillness and clarity, allowing me to align my thoughts and intentions with His divine plan.

These practices are like spiritual nourishment, feeding the depths of my soul and awakening a profound connection to the source of all life. It is through prayer and meditation that I tap into the source of strength and inspiration that empowers me to navigate life's challenges with grace and faith.

I find strength, peace, and purpose in my connection with God.

COLOSSIANS 3:16 (NIV)

"LET THE MESSAGE OF CHRIST DWELL AMONG YOU RICHLY AS YOU TEACH AND ADMONISH ONE ANOTHER WITH ALL WISDOM THROUGH PSALMS, HYMNS, AND SONGS FROM THE SPIRIT, SINGING TO GOD WITH GRATITUDE IN YOUR HEARTS."

His presence in my life is my foundation and my source of unwavering strength during the storms of life. Through Him, I discover the peace that surpasses all understanding, a calm amid chaos.

It is in His guidance that I uncover my true purpose, a divine calling that fills my heart with meaning and fulfillment. My relationship with God is the fountain of my existence, a constant reminder that I am never alone on this journey.

In His embrace, I find the courage to face any challenge and the assurance that His plan for my life is greater than anything I could ever imagine.

In God's light, I discover my true path and calling.

ROMANS 12:12 (NIV)

"BE JOYFUL IN HOPE, PATIENT IN AFFLICTION, FAITHFUL IN PRAYER."

His divine illumination guides my steps, revealing the purpose He has intricately woven into the fabric of my being. It is in His radiant presence that I find clarity amidst life's uncertainties, and His light dispels the shadows of doubt and fear.

With each step I take along this illuminated path, I walk closer to the destiny He has ordained for me. I trust that His light will always guide me, even in the darkest of moments, and that by following His divine glow, I will fulfill the unique calling He has placed upon my life.

I commit to nurturing my relationship with God with devotion.

1 THESSALONIANS 5:16-18 (NIV)

"REJOICE ALWAYS, PRAY CONTINUALLY, GIVE THANKS IN ALL CIRCUMSTANCES; FOR THIS IS GOD'S WILL FOR YOU IN CHRIST JESUS."

Just like a gardener tends to the most delicate and precious of blossoms, I cultivate my connection with the divine. Through prayer, worship, and heartfelt conversations, I create a sacred space where God's presence can flourish within my soul.

My commitment to devotion is a testament to my desire to know Him deeply, to listen for His wisdom, and to align my heart with His divine purpose. In this sacred partnership, I find strength, solace, and unwavering guidance, for I know that in His presence, my soul truly thrives.

I am transformed, guided, and protected by my connection with God.

ACTS 17:27 (NIV)

"GOD DID THIS SO THAT THEY WOULD SEEK HIM AND PERHAPS REACH OUT FOR HIM AND FIND HIM, THOUGH HE IS NOT FAR FROM ANY ONE OF US."

Each day, I open my heart to His divine presence and the immense power of His love. His transformative grace molds me into the best version of myself, guiding my steps and illuminating my path.

In His presence, I find shelter from life's storms, knowing that His protective embrace shields me from harm. With God by my side, I am strengthened, guided, and protected, walking the journey of life with unwavering faith and the assurance that His love is my greatest source of transformation and security.

Every moment spent with God brings me closer to the best version of myself.

PSALM 95:6 (NIV)

"COME, LET US BOW DOWN IN WORSHIP, LET US KNEEL BEFORE THE LORD OUR MAKER."

In the stillness of His presence, I discover profound insights and revelations that guide my steps toward greater purpose and fulfillment. Each prayer, each meditation, each connection with the Divine nourishes my soul and deepens my understanding of His plan for my life.

I am continually transformed, shaped, and refined as I seek His wisdom and love. With each passing moment, I become more aligned with His purpose, more attuned to His will, and more aware of the incredible journey of self-discovery and growth that unfolds in His presence.

Let your Life be affirmed

October:

Unafraid To Fail and Ready To Fly

Shifting Your Mindset About Failure and The Reality of What It Means to Fail

In this chapter, we explore the transformational power of failure on our journey toward personal and professional growth. Rather than fearing failure, view it as a valuable teacher who imparts lessons far more profound than success ever could. By adapting a healthy and comfortable relationship with failure, it becomes the steppingstone to greater accomplishments, provided we approach it with a spirit of resilience and unwavering faith.

If you talk to any successful person, if they are honest, they will tell you that they learned more from failing than they ever did from succeeding. This is by divine design; because in making mistakes, we learn what works and what does not work. If we frame it properly, it can also help to build our confidence, empowering us to move forward with no loss of enthusiasm and enhanced insights and wisdom.

This month, get comfortable with failing. And reframe past failures as lessons that have catapulted you to where you are right now.

Failure does not scare me; it is simply my internal GPS rerouting me in the proper direction.

PROVERBS 24:16 (NIV)

"FOR THOUGH THE RIGHTEOUS FALL SEVEN TIMES, THEY RISE AGAIN, BUT THE WICKED STUMBLE WHEN CALAMITY STRIKES."

I embrace each setback as an opportunity for growth and learning. It's in moments of adversity that I discover my true resilience and strength. God's guidance and love lead me through every challenge, reminding me that He has a purpose for my life that transcends any temporary setbacks.

With faith as my compass and perseverance as my driving force, I trust that failure is not an end but a necessary part of the journey toward my divine destiny.

I embrace failure as a steppingstone to success.

PSALM 37:5 (NIV)

"COMMIT YOUR WAY TO THE LORD; TRUST IN HIM AND HE WILL DO THIS."

Rather than fearing or avoiding it, I understand that failure is a natural part of any movement toward greatness. Every stumble or setback is an opportunity to learn, grow, become better, stronger, and even more committed to my goals.

Through these learning experiences, I gain wisdom, resilience, and a deeper understanding of myself and my purpose. With God's guidance, I transform failure into a powerful catalyst for progress, knowing that each stumble brings me one step closer to achieving my dreams and living out His divine plan for my life.

Failure is my teacher, and I am an eager learner.

2 TIMOTHY 2:15 (NIV)

"DO YOUR BEST TO PRESENT YOURSELF TO GOD AS ONE APPROVED, A WORKER WHO DOES NOT NEED TO BE ASHAMED AND WHO CORRECTLY HANDLES THE WORD OF TRUTH."

I approach each setback with an open heart and a willing spirit, knowing that in every moment of adversity, there is a valuable lesson awaiting discovery. With faith as my guide, I view failures not as obstacles but as opportunities for growth and transformation.

God's wisdom and grace shine through every challenge, helping me to navigate life's difficulties with courage and resilience. I am grateful for the lessons I've learned from my failures, for they have equipped me to rise stronger, wiser, and more determined to fulfill my purpose as I walk in His light.

I see every setback as a setup for a comeback.

PSALM 34:4 (NIV)

"I SOUGHT THE LORD, AND HE ANSWERED ME; HE DELIVERED ME FROM ALL MY FEARS."

When life takes unexpected turns, I hold onto my belief in God's promises, trusting that He has a greater plan in store for me. Adversity is not the end of my story; it's a temporary pause that prepares me for a triumphant return.

With faith as my compass, I navigate through challenges, for they are shaping me into a stronger, more resilient individual. God's grace and guidance illuminate the path forward, reminding me that setbacks are simply steppingstones leading to a brighter and more purposeful future.

I embrace each setback with hope and determination, for I trust in God's divine plan for my life.

I am resilient, and failure cannot deter my spirit.

PSALM 56:3 (NIV)

"WHEN I AM AFRAID, I PUT MY TRUST IN YOU."

I rise above setbacks and obstacles with determination and faith. Failure is not a reflection of my worth but a slight detour on my success path. Each challenge I encounter brings knowledge, growth, trust, and strength.

I tap into my inner strength and faith, knowing that I have the power to overcome any adversity that comes my way.

Failure may slow me down, but it can never break my spirit or diminish my resolve. I embrace it as a steppingstone to achieving my goals and fulfilling my purpose.

Mistakes do not define me; my response to them does.

ISAIAH 40:31 (NIV)

"BUT THOSE WHO HOPE IN THE LORD WILL RENEW THEIR STRENGTH. THEY WILL SOAR ON WINGS LIKE EAGLES; THEY WILL RUN AND NOT GROW WEARY, THEY WILL WALK AND NOT BE FAINT."

When I make errors or face setbacks, I choose to respond with grace, resilience, and a commitment to growth. Making mistakes is a natural part of life, and they provide valuable lessons that shape my character and wisdom.

Rather than dwelling on my errors, I focus on how I can learn from them and become a better version of myself. I embrace the self-improvement that mistakes offer, knowing that my response to challenges and setbacks ultimately determines my path to success and fulfillment.

I am not afraid to fail, for it leads me closer to my goals.

PSALM 40:1-2 (NIV)

"I WAITED PATIENTLY FOR THE LORD; HE TURNED TO ME AND HEARD MY CRY. HE LIFTED ME OUT OF THE SLIMY PIT, OUT OF THE MUD AND MIRE; HE SET MY FEET ON A ROCK AND GAVE ME A FIRM PLACE TO STAND."

Failure is not a barrier but a bridge on my journey to success. Each time I face a setback or stumble, I view it as a re-visioning strategy towards my aspirations. I recognize that some of life's most valuable lessons are learned through adversity.

Instead of fearing failure, I embrace it with courage and determination so that it can provide me with valuable experiences and wisdom that propel me forward on the path to achieving my dreams.

Failure is not final; it's the beginning of my comeback story.

PROVERBS 3:5-6 (NIV)

"TRUST IN THE LORD WITH ALL YOUR HEART AND LEAN NOT ON YOUR OWN UNDERSTANDING; IN ALL YOUR WAYS SUBMIT TO HIM, AND HE WILL MAKE YOUR PATHS STRAIGHT."

When setbacks occur, I don't dwell on them as permanent defeats. Instead, I see them as invitations to tap into a higher level of knowledge and perseverance. Just as the darkest hour precedes dawn, my failures pave the way for my future successes.

I draw strength from the belief that each setback is a chapter in my life's book, and it's up to me to write the next pages with determination and a positive mindset. I refuse to be defined by my failures, but rather, I use them as avenues toward a brighter and more triumphant future.

I use failure as fuel to ignite my determination.

MATTHEW 19:26 (NIV)

"JESUS LOOKED AT THEM AND SAID, "WITH MAN, THIS IS IMPOSSIBLE, BUT WITH GOD ALL THINGS ARE POSSIBLE."

When faced with setbacks and obstacles, I don't allow them to deter me. Instead, I harness the energy of failure to propel me forward. I know God is with me, guiding me every step of the way.

It's in the face of adversity that my faith in God shines the brightest. I understand that every challenge is an opportunity in disguise, and I seize it with unwavering resolve.

Failure becomes a powerful motivator, reminding me of my goals and pushing me to work harder and smarter. I refuse to let fear of failure hold me back because I know that my determination can overcome any obstacle in my path.

I grow stronger with every challenge I face.

ROMANS 15:13 (NIV)

"MAY THE GOD OF HOPE FILL YOU WITH ALL JOY AND PEACE AS YOU TRUST IN HIM, SO THAT YOU MAY OVERFLOW WITH HOPE BY THE POWER OF THE HOLY SPIRIT."

Challenges are not setbacks; they are launching pads for my purpose and destiny. Each challenge I face will strengthen me on my journey of growth and self-improvement.

Each obstacle I encounter presents an opportunity for me to become more resilient, more resourceful, and more determined. I embrace challenges as a chance to learn, adapt, and thrive.

With each challenge conquered, I emerge stronger, more confident, and better equipped to face whatever comes my way.

I am not afraid of challenges; I welcome them with open arms, knowing that they are catalysts for my personal and professional development.

Success is born from the ashes of failure.

PSALM 37:7 (NIV)

"BE STILL BEFORE THE LORD AND WAIT PATIENTLY FOR HIM; DO NOT FRET WHEN PEOPLE SUCCEED IN THEIR WAYS, WHEN THEY CARRY OUT THEIR WICKED SCHEMES."

Just as a phoenix rises from its own ashes, I, too, rise, stronger and more determined when faced with failure. Failure is not the end of my journey but a mile marker, bringing valuable lessons, revelations, and experiences that shape me into the person I am meant to be.

I do not fear failure; I embrace it as a necessary chapter in the book of my success story. With each setback, I learn, grow, and refine my approach. I use failure as a powerful tool to fuel my determination, inspire innovation, and achieve the success I desire.

I am confident that every failure brings me closer to the greatness that awaits me.

I am not limited by my failures; I am propelled by them.

HEBREWS 11:6 (NIV)

"AND WITHOUT FAITH, IT IS IMPOSSIBLE TO PLEASE GOD, BECAUSE ANYONE WHO COMES TO HIM MUST BELIEVE THAT HE EXISTS AND THAT HE REWARDS THOSE WHO EARNESTLY SEEK HIM."

Each failure serves as a launching pad for my growth and success. Instead of allowing failures to hold me back, I use them to spring forward with even greater determination.

My mindset is one of continuous improvement and persistence, so I RSVP "yes" to setbacks so that I learn, adapt, and evolve. I recognize that failure is a natural part of any journey toward success.

By embracing failure and leveraging it as a source of motivation and wisdom, I am empowered to overcome obstacles and achieve my goals with confidence and tenacity.

I am not discouraged by temporary setbacks; I am propelled forward.

1 CORINTHIANS 10:13 (NIV)

"NO TEMPTATION HAS OVERTAKEN YOU EXCEPT WHAT IS COMMON TO MANKIND. AND GOD IS FAITHFUL; HE WILL NOT LET YOU BE TEMPTED BEYOND WHAT YOU CAN BEAR."

When faced with challenges or obstacles, I view them as necessary stops along my path to success. I understand that setbacks are part of any journey, but I refuse to let them define me or deter my progress. Instead, I use setbacks as opportunities for growth and learning.

I remain resilient and focused on my goals, knowing that every setback brings me one step closer to my ultimate destination and the best version of myself. I am determined, driven, and unwavering in my pursuit of success.

I emerge stronger, more experienced, closer to God, and more prepared to conquer whatever lies ahead.

I embrace the challenges that come my way, confident in my ability to turn them into guideposts toward a brighter future.

I learn from my failures and apply those lessons to my journey.

PSALM 121:1-2 (NIV)

"A SONG OF ASCENTS. I LIFT UP MY EYES TO THE MOUNTAINS—WHERE DOES MY HELP COME FROM? MY HELP COMES FROM THE LORD, THE MAKER OF HEAVEN AND EARTH."

Failure is not the end; it's a valuable teacher. When I face setbacks or make mistakes, I don't dwell on them in despair. Instead, I pause, reflect, and extract wisdom from the experience.

Each failure offers insights into what works and what doesn't. It guides me toward better strategies, sharper skills, and a deeper understanding of my path.

As I move forward, I carry the lessons of the past with me. They serve as a compass, helping me navigate the challenges ahead with greater confidence. Failure becomes a powerful tool in my arsenal, propelling me toward my goals and dreams.

Failure is not the end; it's a chance to start anew with greater wisdom and insight.

PSALM 30:5 (NIV)

"FOR HIS ANGER LASTS ONLY A MOMENT, BUT HIS FAVOR LASTS A LIFETIME; WEEPING MAY STAY FOR THE NIGHT, BUT REJOICING COMES IN THE MORNING."

When I encounter setbacks or make mistakes, I don't view them as permanent roadblocks. Instead, I see them as opportunities to hit the reset button and approach my goals more intelligently.

I take the time to analyze what went wrong and why. This introspection helps me identify areas where I can improve and make more informed decisions moving forward. Failure becomes a valuable teacher, guiding me toward better strategies and actions.

In every setback, I find the seeds of future success. I embrace the lessons learned and apply them to my journey with enthusiasm. With each fresh start, I am more resilient, more determined, and better equipped to overcome challenges. Failure is not a defeat; it's a quick pit stop on the path to my dreams.

My identity is not shaped by the moments when I stumble or fall but rather by the moments when I summon the strength to rise again.

ROMANS 12:12 (NIV)

"BE JOYFUL IN HOPE, PATIENT IN AFFLICTION, FAITHFUL IN PRAYER."

I refuse to let stumbles, falls, and errant pushes define me. Instead, I am defined by my resolve and determination to overcome.

When I face adversity, I don't dwell on the fall, I focus on the rising. I draw upon my inner strength and the lessons learned from past experiences to lift myself. Every time I rise, I become more resilient, more courageous, and more prepared.

I am not limited by my mistakes or missteps; I am propelled forward by the indomitable spirit within me. With each rise, I write a chapter of my story that speaks to my ability to triumph over adversity. I am defined by my resilience, my unwavering faith, and my commitment to keep rising, no matter the circumstances.

In the pursuit of my dreams and goals, I embrace the courage to fail boldly.

2 TIMOTHY 1:7 (NKJV)

"FOR GOD HAS NOT GIVEN US A SPIRIT OF FEAR, BUT OF POWER AND OF LOVE AND OF A SOUND MIND."

I understand that failure is not a reflection of my worth. With each bold endeavor, I may stumble, face setbacks, or encounter challenges, but I refuse to let fear of failure hold me back.

I harness the strength within me to rise again, undeterred by temporary defeats. It's through adversity and setbacks that I grow stronger and wiser. These experiences shape me into the tenacious and determined individual I am meant to be.

Failure is not the end of my story; it's a chapter that provides valuable lessons and opportunities for growth. When I fall, I rise with even greater focus, knowing that my courage to face failure head-on is a testament to my unwavering commitment to my dreams.

I am not defined by my failures, but by my ability to rise from them, stronger and more determined than ever before. I embrace the experience of failing boldly and rising with courage, for it is through this process that I truly discover my strength and potential.

I wholeheartedly welcome failure as an indispensable part of my personal and professional growth.

PSALM 73:26 (NIV)

"MY FLESH AND MY HEART MAY FAIL, BUT GOD IS THE STRENGTH OF MY HEART AND MY PORTION FOREVER."

On life's journey, failures provide me with valuable insights, teach me resilience, and offer opportunities to refine my skills and strategies.

With each failure, I grow wiser and more determined. I do not let the fear of failing deter me from pursuing my dreams and aspirations. I embrace the challenges and uncertainties that come my way, knowing that they are essential for my development.

Failure does not define me; my response to it does. I choose to respond with grace, determination, and a commitment to learning from my mistakes. I see every setback as an invitation to improve, adapt, and succeed.

As I navigate the path of life, I understand that it is not about avoiding failure but about embracing it as a vital part of my journey. I am grateful for the growth and strength that come from my failures, and I eagerly anticipate the success that awaits me on the other side of each setback.

My determination stands unshaken in the face of adversity.

1 PETER 5:10 (NIV)

"AND THE GOD OF ALL GRACE, WHO CALLED YOU TO HIS ETERNAL GLORY IN CHRIST, AFTER YOU HAVE SUFFERED A LITTLE WHILE, WILL HIMSELF RESTORE YOU AND MAKE YOU STRONG, FIRM, AND STEADFAST."

I am unwavering in my commitment to pursuing my goals and dreams, regardless of the challenges that may arise. Adversity is not a deterrent for me; it is a catalyst for my inner strength to shine.

When obstacles and setbacks come my way, I do not falter or lose heart. Instead, I see them as opportunities to prove my resilience and determination. I understand that it is through adversity that I grow stronger, both in character and in my ability to overcome.

I approach challenges with a positive mindset, knowing that every difficulty I encounter is a chance for me to rise higher. I draw upon my unwavering determination as a source of motivation and courage. It fuels my actions and propels me forward on my path to success.

In the face of adversity, I do not waver, and I do not give up. I stand firm in my resolve, knowing that with determination as my companion, I can overcome any obstacle and achieve the greatness that lies ahead.

I use setbacks as fuel to drive me closer to my greater purpose.

ROMANS 5:3-4 (NIV)

"NOT ONLY SO, BUT WE ALSO GLORY IN OUR SUFFERINGS, BECAUSE WE KNOW THAT SUFFERING PRODUCES PERSEVERANCE; PERSEVERANCE, CHARACTER; AND CHARACTER, HOPE."

Setbacks propel me closer to my greater purpose. Each setback I encounter serves as valuable fuel for my determination and ambition.

Setbacks remind me of my resilience and tenacity. They push me to dig deeper within myself, tap into my inner strength, and push forward with greater resolve. I use these experiences to refine my skills, enhance my wisdom, and become more equipped for the path ahead.

In the face of setbacks, I remain unshaken, focused, and determined. I keep my eyes on my greater purpose and use setbacks as the fuel that propels me ever forward on my path to success and fulfillment.

Failure is a test of my commitment; I will not waver.

PSALM 37:23-24 (NIV)

"THE LORD MAKES FIRM THE STEPS OF THE ONE WHO DELIGHTS IN HIM; THOUGH HE MAY STUMBLE, HE WILL NOT FALL, FOR THE LORD UPHOLDS HIM WITH HIS HAND."

Setbacks and difficulties are not signs of weakness but tests of my determination and resolve. My commitment to my dreams and aspirations is unshakeable.

I draw strength from my faith and my purpose. I am resolute in my pursuit of success, and no amount of failure can deter me. When faced with adversity, I double down on my efforts, learn from my mistakes, and adjust my course as needed.

I embrace failure as a teacher, not an obstacle. It sharpens my skills, strengthens my character, and deepens my resolve. My commitment to my dreams is unwavering, and I know that with each test I face, I emerge stronger and more determined than before.

I am unshakeable in my pursuit of success.

PSALM 37:24 (NIV)

"THOUGH HE MAY STUMBLE, HE WILL NOT FALL, FOR THE LORD UPHOLDS HIM WITH HIS HAND."

Challenges may arise, and obstacles may block my path, but I remain resolute and unwavering in my determination to achieve my goals. Success is not just a destination for me; it's a goal, and I understand that the road may be fraught with difficulties.

When faced with adversity, I do not crumble; I rise. I draw strength from within, from my faith, from my purpose, and from the unwavering belief that I can achieve great things. I refuse to be swayed by doubt or fear. I use challenges as steppingstones to reach higher and move closer to my goals.

Success requires perseverance, resilience, and an unshakeable spirit. I possess all these qualities and more. I am not deterred by setbacks or failures; I am motivated by them. Each obstacle I encounter only strengthens my resolve and propels me forward.

OCTOBER 23

Failure is not an end; it is a beginning.

PSALM 51:10 (NIV)

"CREATE IN ME A PURE HEART, O GOD, AND RENEW A STEADFAST SPIRIT WITHIN ME."

Every failure in my life is not a dead end but a seed waiting to sprout into my success story. I understand that setbacks and mistakes are not roadblocks but green flags ushering me to learn, grow, and ultimately flourish.

With faith in God's plan for me and unwavering determination, I nurture these seeds of failure, knowing that they hold the potential to bear the sweetest fruits of success.

Every stumble is a step toward my destiny, and I embrace each one with gratitude, for it brings me closer to the fulfillment of my purpose.

I turn obstacles into opportunities.

LAMENTATIONS 3:22-23 (NIV)

"BECAUSE OF THE LORD'S GREAT LOVE WE ARE NOT CONSUMED, FOR HIS COMPASSIONS NEVER FAIL. THEY ARE NEW EVERY MORNING; GREAT IS YOUR FAITHFULNESS."

I passionately believe that obstacles in my path are invitations to discover hidden opportunities. With unwavering faith and a mindset rooted in God, I approach challenges as His guidance, gently moving me toward my greater purpose.

By seeking His wisdom and relying on His strength, I am empowered to turn even the most daunting obstacles into catalysts of growth, resilience, and achievement.

With God by my side, I transform adversity into a powerful catalyst for my success and personal transformation.

I am not discouraged by temporary defeats; I am inspired by future victories.

2 CORINTHIANS 12:9 (NIV)

"BUT HE SAID TO ME, 'MY GRACE IS SUFFICIENT FOR YOU, FOR MY POWER IS MADE PERFECT IN WEAKNESS.' THEREFORE I WILL BOAST ALL THE MORE GLADLY ABOUT MY WEAKNESSES, SO THAT CHRIST'S POWER MAY REST ON ME."

I am so glad that God loves me enough to give me grace. Temporary defeats may test my resolve, but because of God's unchanging love, they will never deter my spirit.

I draw inspiration from the knowledge that every setback is merely a setup for a comeback. With my faith firmly anchored in God's plan, I embrace the challenges that come my way, knowing that they are shaping me for future victories. I view these moments as opportunities for growth, learning, and becoming better equipped to fulfill my purpose.

With God's unyielding support, I am not discouraged by temporary defeats; instead, I am inspired to press on toward the abundant victories that await me in His plan.

I am not defeated by failure; I am energized by it.

ISAIAH 41:10 (NIV)

"SO DO NOT FEAR, FOR I AM WITH YOU; DO NOT BE DISMAYED, FOR I AM YOUR GOD. I WILL STRENGTHEN YOU AND HELP YOU; I WILL UPHOLD YOU WITH MY RIGHTEOUS RIGHT HAND."

Failure is not my adversary; it is my ally. I understand that in the face of failure, I am presented with a remarkable opportunity for growth and transformation.

With faith in God's purpose for my life, I harness the energy that arises from setbacks. I use failure as a catalyst, fueling my determination and propelling me toward my goals.

Instead of defeat, I find empowerment in the lessons learned, and the strength gained through adversity. Failure is not the end of my journey; it is a crucial part of my path to success, a path I walk with resilience and an indomitable spirit.

I am a master at turning setbacks into set ups for blessings.

JAMES 1:2-4 (NIV)

"CONSIDER IT PURE JOY, MY BROTHERS, AND SISTERS, WHENEVER YOU FACE TRIALS OF MANY KINDS BECAUSE YOU KNOW THAT THE TESTING OF YOUR FAITH PRODUCES PERSEVERANCE."

Setbacks may try to knock me down, but they don't stand a chance against my faith and determination. I've honed the skill of turning setbacks into divine setups for blessings, just as God has called me to.

In every challenge, I see an opportunity for God to work miracles in my life. I trust that even when things don't go as planned, they are simply aligning with a greater purpose. With this perspective, I embrace setbacks as God's unchanging hand, gently pushing me toward the abundant blessings that He has in store for me.

I am a master at transforming adversity into advancement, and I walk my path with grace and gratitude, knowing that every setback is simply a setup for God's abundant grace to shine through.

I rise above failure, stronger and wiser than before.

PHILIPPIANS 4:13 (NKJV)

"I CAN DO ALL THINGS THROUGH CHRIST WHO STRENGTHENS ME."

Failure is not my end; it's a powerful catalyst for growth and transformation. Each time I face failure, I rise above it, like a phoenix from the ashes, stronger and wiser than before.

Failure becomes an opportunity for a new beginning, a source of strength, resilience, and wisdom. I understand that my life is not about avoiding failure but about embracing it as a vital part of my path toward becoming the best version of myself.

With faith and perseverance, I continually rise above, knowing that failure is a temporary setback on the road to my ultimate victory.

I am not limited by my past failures; I am empowered by them.

ROMANS 8:28 (NIV)

"AND WE KNOW THAT IN ALL THINGS GOD WORKS FOR THE GOOD OF THOSE WHO LOVE HIM, WHO HAVE BEEN CALLED ACCORDING TO HIS PURPOSE."

I refuse to let my past failures define or limit me. Instead, I choose to see them as valuable lessons on my road toward success. These failures have equipped me with the wisdom, strength, and resilience needed to overcome any challenge that lies ahead.

They are not roadblocks; they are opportunities for growth and transformation. As I embrace my past failures with faith and determination, I am empowered to rise above them and reach new heights in every aspect of my life.

My past does not dictate my future; I am the author of my own story, empowered by every chapter, including the ones marked by failure.

I am fueled by the fire of determination, not hindered by the fear of failure.

2 CORINTHIANS 4:16-18 (ESV)

"SO WE DO NOT LOSE HEART. THOUGH OUR OUTER SELF IS WASTING AWAY, OUR INNER SELF IS BEING RENEWED DAY BY DAY. FOR THIS LIGHT MOMENTARY AFFLICTION IS PREPARING FOR US AN ETERNAL WEIGHT OF GLORY BEYOND ALL COMPARISON, AS WE LOOK NOT TO THE THINGS THAT ARE SEEN BUT TO THE THINGS THAT ARE UNSEEN. FOR THE THINGS THAT ARE SEEN ARE TRANSIENT, BUT THE THINGS THAT ARE UNSEEN ARE ETERNAL."

I am driven by God's abundant love and an unyielding determination that ignites my path toward success. Instead of being paralyzed by the fear of failure, I use it as fuel to propel me forward.

Failure is not my adversary; it is my teacher guiding me with valuable lessons. Every setback is an opportunity to grow stronger, wiser, and more resolute in my pursuit of my goals.

With faith as my compass and determination as my driving force, I move fearlessly toward my aspirations, knowing that each step, even those marred by challenges, leads me closer to victory.

Failure is my launching pad to greatness. I am destined for success.

MICAH 7:7 (BSB)

"BUT AS FOR ME, I WILL LOOK TO THE LORD; I WILL WAIT FOR THE GOD OF MY SALVATION; MY GOD WILL HEAR ME."

Failures, disappointments, unexpected outcomes, and detours serve as my launching pads to greatness. It is through the lessons learned in the face of setbacks that I discover my true potential.

I am destined for success, and every failure is full of lessons, expanding my mind and helping me to grow. With relentless faith, determination, and a resilient spirit, I rise above adversity, knowing that each experience, no matter how challenging, prepares me for the greatness that awaits.

I embrace failure as a companion on this remarkable voyage toward a future filled with achievement and purpose.

Let your Life be affirmed

November:

Growing In Gratitude

Unlocking The Secret to True Joy and Fulfillment

In the journey of life, one of the most transformative virtues we can nurture is gratitude. Gratitude has opened doors for me that still leave me completely flabbergasted. Cultivating a heart of gratitude is not just a pleasant sentiment but a powerful mindset shift that can profoundly impact our lives. This month, I challenge you to get radical and intentional about walking in gratitude.

Gratitude is not merely a response to blessings but a posture of the heart that can transcend any trial or tribulation. It's an acknowledgment of God's goodness, even amid challenging times. By fostering an attitude of gratitude, we shift our focus from what we lack to what we have, opening our hearts to receive God's blessings with humility and appreciation.

A heart filled with gratitude has the potential to transform every aspect of our lives. Being grateful deepens our connection with God. By acknowledging the abundance of blessings we've received, we become more content and resilient in the face of adversity. Gratitude is a reminder that God's grace is always sufficient, and this mindset shift can lead to increased happiness, improved relationships, and a sense of purpose that transcends our circumstances.

This month's affirmations focus on small ways that you can embody gratitude every day. By living a life marked by gratitude, we not only draw closer to God but also inspire and uplift those around us. You don't have to wait for Thanksgiving to give thanks. Give thanks every day that you are alive.

I am grateful for the gift of life, and I cherish every moment.

REVELATION 11:17 (NIV)

"WE GIVE THANKS TO YOU, LORD GOD ALMIGHTY, THE ONE WHO IS AND WHO WAS BECAUSE YOU HAVE TAKEN YOUR GREAT POWER AND HAVE BEGUN TO REIGN."

I am grateful for the precious gift of life that God has bestowed upon me, and I hold each moment in deep reverence. Life is a beautiful tapestry of experiences, both joys and challenges, and it's through gratitude that I find the richness in every moment.

I cherish the opportunities to grow, to love, and to make a positive impact on this world. Every breath I take is a reminder of God's grace, and I am determined to live each day with a heart overflowing with gratitude, embracing life's beauty with open arms.

Gratitude is the foundation of my happiness, and I cultivate it daily.

PSALM 95:1 (NIV)

"COME, LET US SING FOR JOY TO THE LORD; LET US SHOUT ALOUD TO THE ROCK OF OUR SALVATION."

Gratitude is the bedrock upon which my happiness is built, and I make it a daily practice to nurture this essential virtue. Each morning, I wake up with a heart filled with thankfulness for the gift of a new day. I am mindful of the countless blessings that surround me – from the love of family and friends to the simple pleasures of life.

Through the practice of gratitude, I am not only reminded of God's abundant goodness but also empowered to face each day with a positive mindset and a joyful spirit.

It is in this state of thankfulness that I find the true essence of happiness, and I continue to cultivate it as a guiding light in my life.

I find joy in the simple pleasures of life and appreciate them fully.

PSALM 107:22 (NIV)

"LET THEM SACRIFICE THANK OFFERINGS AND TELL OF HIS WORKS WITH SONGS OF JOY."

I wholeheartedly embrace the simple pleasures of life and relish them with a deep sense of appreciation and joy. In the gentle whisper of a morning breeze, the warmth of sunlight on my face, the laughter of loved ones, and the beauty of nature's wonders, I discover an abundance of happiness. These seemingly small moments are, in fact, the building blocks of a fulfilling life.

By savoring each simple pleasure and acknowledging the divine grace within them, I can find boundless joy in the everyday experiences that surround me.

Life's beauty lies not only in grand moments but also in the tapestry of these simple, precious gifts, and I cherish them with a heart overflowing with gratitude.

I express gratitude to the people who love and support me.

PSALM 26:7 (NIV)

"PROCLAIMING ALOUD YOUR PRAISE AND TELLING OF ALL YOUR WONDERFUL DEEDS."

I am deeply grateful for the incredible people who surround me with love and support. Their presence in my life is a precious gift that fills my heart with warmth and gratitude.

Whether it's family members who have stood by me through thick and thin, friends who have shared laughter and tears, or mentors who have guided and inspired me, I recognize the profound impact they have on my journey.

My heart overflows with thankfulness for these cherished relationships, and I make it a point to express my gratitude and love to them regularly. Their love is a beacon of light, and I am truly blessed to have them as part of my life's tapestry.

I am thankful for the challenges I face, as they make me stronger.

1 CHRONICLES 16:8 (NIV)

"GIVE PRAISE TO THE LORD, PROCLAIM HIS NAME; MAKE KNOWN AMONG THE NATIONS WHAT HE HAS DONE."

I embrace challenges as opportunities for growth and transformation. Every obstacle I encounter becomes inspiration on my journey towards becoming the best version of myself.

Challenges may test my resilience, but they also reveal the depth of my inner strength. I am thankful for these trials because they shape me into a stronger, wiser, and more resilient individual.

With faith as my guide, I navigate through challenges with a heart full of gratitude, knowing that each hurdle I overcome brings me one step closer to my divine purpose.

Gratitude fills my heart and radiates positivity in all I do.

PSALM 50:23 (NIV)

"THOSE WHO SACRIFICE THANK OFFERINGS HONOR ME, AND TO THE BLAMELESS, I WILL SHOW MY SALVATION."

Gratitude is the radiant light that fills my heart and infuses positivity into every facet of my life. It's the attitude I carry with me, coloring my actions, words, and thoughts with a joyful hue.

As I express gratitude daily, it becomes a powerful force that transforms my perspective, attracting more blessings and goodness into my life. Gratitude is not just a feeling; it's a way of life, a faith that allows me to navigate life's journey with grace and optimism.

With a heart brimming with thankfulness, I create a ripple effect of positivity, touching the lives of those around me and shining a light on the path to a brighter, more fulfilling future.

I count my blessings every day and am overwhelmed by their abundance.

ROMANS 1:21 (NIV)

"FOR ALTHOUGH THEY KNEW GOD, THEY NEITHER GLORIFIED HIM AS GOD NOR GAVE THANKS TO HIM, BUT THEIR THINKING BECAME FUTILE, AND THEIR FOOLISH HEARTS WERE DARKENED."

Each day, as I count my blessings, I am overwhelmed by their sheer abundance. My heart swells with gratitude as I recognize the countless gifts that grace my life. From the warmth of cherished relationships to the simplest daily living pleasures, I find myself surrounded by a sea of blessings.

My practice of gratitude fills me with a profound sense of contentment and reminds me that even in the midst of life's challenges, there is an abundance of goodness found in God's will.

I am truly humbled by the richness of life's tapestry, woven together by the threads of God's grace and love.

I embrace each new day with a heart full of gratitude and optimism.

PSALM 116:17 (NIV)

"I WILL SACRIFICE A THANK OFFERING TO YOU AND CALL ON THE NAME OF THE LORD."

As I awaken to the dawn of a new day, I embrace it with a heart full of gratitude and boundless optimism. With each sunrise, the precious gift of life and the opportunity for a fresh start greet me.

Gratitude flows through me like a river, washing away any remnants of negativity and doubt. I choose to focus on the beauty that surrounds me, the love that fills my life, and the endless possibilities that await.

This attitude of gratitude and optimism propels me forward, ready to seize the day with enthusiasm, knowing that every moment is a chance to experience God's grace and create a brighter future.

I find beauty in the world around me and am thankful for its wonders.

REVELATION 7:12 (NIV)

"AMEN! PRAISE AND GLORY AND WISDOM AND THANKS AND HONOR AND POWER AND STRENGTH BE TO OUR GOD FOR EVER AND EVER. AMEN!"

I discover boundless beauty in the world around me and am continually grateful for its wonders. Whether it's the delicate petals of a blooming flower, the majestic hues of a sunset painting the sky, or the harmonious laughter of loved ones, I can enjoy the masterpiece that is God's creation.

Each day, I make it a point to pause, take in the magnificence that surrounds me, and offer thanks for the visual and sensory treasures that enrich my life.

This practice of finding beauty in the world and expressing gratitude fills my soul with joy and deepens my connection to the Creator, who paints such breathtaking pictures in our lives every day.

I am grateful for the opportunities that come my way, and I seize them with enthusiasm.

PSALM 28:7 (NIV)

"THE LORD IS MY STRENGTH AND MY SHIELD; MY HEART TRUSTS IN HIM, AND HE HELPS ME. MY HEART LEAPS FOR JOY, AND WITH MY SONG, I PRAISE HIM."

I hold a heart filled with gratitude for the opportunities that grace my path, and I embrace them with enthusiasm. Every new door that opens, every challenge that presents itself, and every chance to make a positive impact in the lives of others is a gift from above.

God places these opportunities in my life for a reason, and I approach them with a spirit of determination and joy.

With each endeavor, I am not only thankful for the chance to grow and contribute, but I also recognize that by seizing these moments with enthusiasm, I honor the divine blessings that come my way.

My practice of gratitude attracts more blessings into my life.

2 CORINTHIANS 9:11 (NIV)

"YOU WILL BE ENRICHED IN EVERY WAY SO THAT YOU CAN BE GENEROUS ON EVERY OCCASION, AND THROUGH US, YOUR GENEROSITY WILL RESULT IN THANKSGIVING TO GOD."

My daily practice of gratitude serves as a powerful magnet, drawing even more blessings into my life. As I express thanks for the abundance that already surrounds me, I send out positive energy into the universe, creating a welcoming space for greater blessings to flow in.

It's like a divine cycle – the more I acknowledge and appreciate the gifts I've received, the more I find myself showered with new opportunities, joy, and love. This practice of gratitude not only enriches my life but also reinforces my faith in God's continuous provision.

I am thankful for my health and wellbeing, and I take care of myself.

2 CORINTHIANS 4:15 (NIV)

"ALL THIS IS FOR YOUR BENEFIT, SO THAT THE GRACE THAT IS REACHING MORE AND MORE PEOPLE MAY CAUSE THANKSGIVING TO OVERFLOW TO THE GLORY OF GOD."

I am deeply thankful for the precious gift of health and wellness that God has entrusted me with, and I honor this gift by taking diligent care of myself. I understand that my physical, emotional, and spiritual wellbeing are interconnected, and I embrace practices that nourish all aspects of my life.

Through daily exercise, mindful nutrition, and nurturing my mental and emotional health, I ensure that I am operating at my best to fulfill my purpose and serve others.

Gratitude for my health motivates me to make choices that align with God's plan for my life, enabling me to thrive and shine my light in the world.

I appreciate the love and laughter shared with my friends and family.

PSALM 50:14 (NIV)

"SACRIFICE THANK OFFERINGS TO GOD, FULFILL YOUR VOWS TO THE MOST HIGH."

I hold in my heart a profound appreciation for the love and laughter that grace my life through the cherished bonds with my friends and family. These relationships are divine blessings that fill my days with warmth and joy.

The moments of togetherness, the shared stories, and the laughter that echoes through our gatherings are treasures I value beyond measure. In their company, I find strength, support, and a deep sense of belonging that fuels my journey.

Through gratitude for these precious connections, I recognize the love of God weaving through every thread of my life, enriching my existence with love and laughter that light up my path.

I am thankful for the lessons I learn from both success and setbacks.

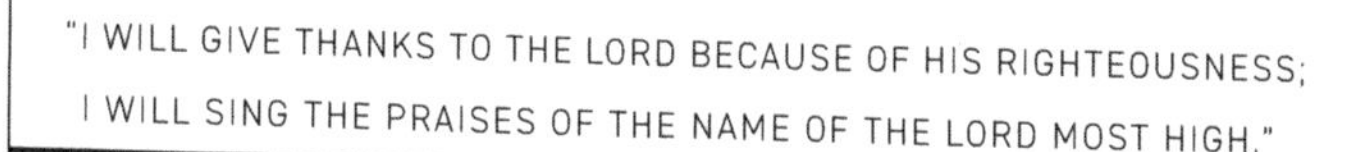

PSALM 7:17 (NIV)

"I WILL GIVE THANKS TO THE LORD BECAUSE OF HIS RIGHTEOUSNESS; I WILL SING THE PRAISES OF THE NAME OF THE LORD MOST HIGH."

I embrace each lesson that comes my way, whether in the embrace of success or the challenges of setbacks. Every experience, whether it leads to triumph or teaches me resilience, holds invaluable wisdom.

Success reminds me of my potential, while setbacks guide me toward growth and refinement. In gratitude for these lessons, I find the strength to persevere and the wisdom to navigate life's ever-unfolding chapters.

Both success and setbacks shape me into a stronger, wiser, and more compassionate version of myself, and for that, I am profoundly thankful.

Gratitude is the key to unlocking a life of abundance and fulfillment.

1 CHRONICLES 29:13 (NIV)

"NOW, OUR GOD, WE GIVE YOU THANKS, AND PRAISE YOUR GLORIOUS NAME."

Gratitude is indeed the key that unlocks the doors to abundance and fulfillment in life. When we cultivate a heart of gratitude, we open ourselves to the countless blessings that surround us daily. It shifts our perspective, allowing us to see beauty in the simplest of moments and appreciate the richness of our experiences.

Through gratitude, we attract positivity, create a joyful atmosphere, and invite more blessings into our lives. It's a powerful force that aligns us with the divine and reminds us that even in challenging times, there is always something to be thankful for.

Gratitude paves the way for a life filled with abundance, contentment, and a deep sense of fulfillment.

I am grateful for the wisdom that comes with each passing day.

PSALM 118:21 (NIV)

"I WILL GIVE YOU THANKS, FOR YOU ANSWERED ME; YOU HAVE BECOME MY SALVATION."

I embrace each new day with a heart brimming with gratitude for the wisdom it brings. With every sunrise, I am gifted the opportunity to learn, grow, and gain valuable insights.

The experiences, challenges, and moments of clarity that come my way are all precious teachers, enriching my journey. I am thankful for the wisdom that unfolds before me, guiding me toward a life filled with purpose and understanding.

Each passing day is a reminder that with an open heart and a receptive spirit, I can continue to evolve and become the best version of myself.

I radiate positivity and gratitude, attracting positivity into my life.

HEBREWS 12:28 (NIV)

"THEREFORE, SINCE WE ARE RECEIVING A KINGDOM THAT CANNOT BE SHAKEN, LET US BE THANKFUL, AND SO WORSHIP GOD ACCEPTABLY WITH REVERENCE AND AWE."

I radiate positivity and gratitude like a beacon, and in doing so, I invite boundless positivity into my life. By maintaining a grateful heart and focusing on the bright side of every situation, I create an environment of optimism that draws in more blessings.

This cycle of positivity is a powerful force, guiding me toward a life filled with joy, abundance, and fulfillment. As I continue to cultivate this mindset of gratitude, I watch as it transforms not only my own life but also the lives of those I touch with my positivity and warmth.

I am thankful for the gift of forgiveness, which brings inner peace.

PSALM 69:30 (NIV)

"I WILL PRAISE GOD'S NAME IN SONG AND GLORIFY HIM WITH THANKSGIVING."

I am profoundly thankful for the precious gift of forgiveness, a divine blessing that bestows upon me the gift of inner peace. Through forgiveness, I release the burdens of resentment and anger, freeing my heart from the weight of past transgressions.

As I embrace forgiveness, I experience a profound sense of serenity and liberation, knowing that God's grace extends to both the forgiver and the forgiven.

It is through this act of grace and mercy that I find solace and harmony within myself, forging a path to greater spiritual growth and understanding.

I express gratitude for the present moment, savoring it fully.

1 TIMOTHY 4:4-5 (NIV)

"FOR EVERYTHING GOD CREATED IS GOOD, AND NOTHING IS TO BE REJECTED IF IT IS RECEIVED WITH THANKSGIVING BECAUSE IT IS CONSECRATED BY THE WORD OF GOD AND PRAYER."

Each day, I make a conscious choice to express heartfelt gratitude for the present moment, savoring it in all its richness. In this moment, I find a wellspring of joy, peace, and contentment. I understand that life unfolds in the here and now, and by embracing it with a thankful heart, I extract its full essence and beauty.

I am keenly aware that the present is a gift from God, and I unwrap it with reverence, allowing its blessings to cascade over me and infuse my life with positivity and purpose. This practice of cherishing the present moment deepens my connection with the divine and enhances my overall wellbeing.

I am thankful for the power of choice in creating my reality.

PSALM 30:12 (NIV)

"THAT MY HEART MAY SING YOUR PRAISES AND NOT BE SILENT. LORD MY GOD, I WILL PRAISE YOU FOREVER."

I am profoundly thankful for the incredible power of choice that resides within me. Each decision I make, whether big or small, shapes my reality and paves the path toward my dreams. I recognize that this power is a divine gift, a reflection of God's love for me.

With each choice, I am co-creating my destiny, aligning my life with His purpose. I approach each day with gratitude for the opportunity to make choices that lead me toward a future filled with abundance, joy, and fulfillment.

Through the grace of God and the choices I make, I am the author of my own story, and I am eternally grateful for this precious privilege.

Gratitude is my daily practice, and it transforms my life.

1 CHRONICLES 16:34 (NIV)

"GIVE THANKS TO THE LORD, FOR HE IS GOOD; HIS LOVE ENDURES FOREVER."

Gratitude is not just a fleeting emotion for me; it is my steadfast daily practice that holds the power to transform every aspect of my life. Each morning, I begin my day with a heart full of thanks, acknowledging the countless blessings that surround me.

This practice sets a positive tone, infusing my actions, thoughts, and interactions with a radiant sense of appreciation. I believe that in the practice of gratitude, I invite more blessings, joy, and abundance into my life, creating a ripple effect of positivity that touches everyone I encounter.

It is through this transformative practice that I continually discover the extraordinary in the ordinary, making each day a gift to cherish and celebrate.

I am grateful for the diversity and beauty of the world we share.

PSALM 9:1 (NIV)

"FOR THE DIRECTOR OF MUSIC. TO THE TUNE OF "THE DEATH OF THE SON." A PSALM OF DAVID. I WILL GIVE THANKS TO YOU, LORD, WITH ALL MY HEART; I WILL TELL OF ALL YOUR WONDERFUL DEEDS."

In the tapestry of life, I find deep gratitude for the rich diversity and unparalleled beauty that our world encompasses. I see the hand of the Divine in the myriad cultures, landscapes, and people that grace this planet.

It's a reminder that each day is a unique opportunity to learn, connect, and appreciate the differences that make our world vibrant and harmonious.

Through gratitude, I open my heart to the wonders of this diverse tapestry, finding unity in our shared humanity and rejoicing in the breathtaking beauty that surrounds us.

I find thankfulness in both the journey and the destination.

EPHESIANS 5:20 (NIV)

"ALWAYS GIVING THANKS TO GOD THE FATHER FOR EVERYTHING, IN THE NAME OF OUR LORD JESUS CHRIST."

In the grand adventure of life, I've discovered the profound wisdom in finding thankfulness not only at the destination but also along the journey itself.

Every step, every twist, and every turn in my path has purpose and meaning. Each moment is an opportunity to learn, grow, and appreciate the intricate beauty of the process.

While reaching my goals and destinations is fulfilling, I've learned that true richness lies in being grateful for the challenges that strengthen me, the lessons that mold me, and the joys that light my way.

With a heart full of gratitude, I embrace both the path and the arrival, knowing that every moment is a precious gift from above.

My heart overflows with gratitude, touching everyone I meet.

PSALM 95:2 (NIV)

"LET US COME BEFORE HIM WITH THANKSGIVING AND EXTOL HIM WITH MUSIC AND SONG."

As I walk through life with a heart overflowing with gratitude, I become a beacon of light to those I encounter along my path. My gratitude spreads positivity, warmth, and love to everyone it touches.

It's not just a personal practice; it's a gift I share with the world. Through my actions, my words, and my demeanor, I inspire others to embrace gratitude in their own lives, creating a ripple effect of joy, kindness, and thankfulness that can transform the lives of those around me.

Gratitude is a powerful force, and I'm grateful for the opportunity to share its beauty with others.

I am thankful for the challenges that help me grow and evolve.

PHILIPPIANS 4:6 (NIV)

"DO NOT BE ANXIOUS ABOUT ANYTHING, BUT IN EVERY SITUATION, BY PRAYER AND PETITION, WITH THANKSGIVING, PRESENT YOUR REQUESTS TO GOD."

I greet each challenge in my life with a heart full of gratitude, knowing that it is through these challenges that I grow and evolve. Just as a tree's roots grow stronger when it faces strong winds, my character and resilience are fortified when I face life's storms.

Challenges are not obstacles but encouragement on my path to becoming the best version of myself. They teach me valuable lessons, reveal my inner strength, and guide me towards my higher purpose.

With gratitude in my heart, I embrace these challenges, for I know they are shaping me into a better and stronger person each day.

Gratitude is a magnet for abundance, and I attract abundance daily.

PSALM 100:4 (NIV)

"ENTER HIS GATES WITH THANKSGIVING AND HIS COURTS WITH PRAISE; GIVE THANKS TO HIM AND PRAISE HIS NAME."

Gratitude is the powerful magnet that draws abundance into my life every day. As I cultivate a heart overflowing with thankfulness, I open the doors of my life to the countless blessings that surround me.

The more I appreciate the abundance already present, the more abundance I attract. This divine law of attraction is at work in my life, bringing prosperity, joy, and opportunities.

With each moment of gratitude, I align myself with the abundance that God has prepared for me, and I welcome it with open arms.

I appreciate the unique gifts and talents that make me who I am.

PSALM 136:26 (NIV)

"GIVE THANKS TO THE GOD OF HEAVEN. HIS LOVE ENDURES FOREVER."

I wholeheartedly appreciate the unique gifts and talents that make me who I am. Each one of us is fearfully and wonderfully made by our Creator, and my individuality is a beautiful blend of God's design.

By embracing and celebrating my unique qualities, I honor the divine craftsmanship that has gone into creating me. I recognize that my strengths, quirks, and abilities are all part of a grand plan, and I cherish them as the tools with which I can make a positive impact in the world.

With gratitude in my heart for the person I am, I step confidently into each day, ready to share my unique gifts with others and fulfill my purpose.

I am grateful for the abundance of love that surrounds me.

COLOSSIANS 3:15 (NIV)

"LET THE PEACE OF CHRIST RULE IN YOUR HEARTS, SINCE AS MEMBERS OF ONE BODY YOU WERE CALLED TO PEACE. AND BE THANKFUL."

I am profoundly grateful for the abundance of love that envelops me daily. Love, the greatest gift of all, flows from the very heart of God and permeates every aspect of my life. It's in the warm embrace of family and friends, the kindness of strangers, and the beauty of nature.

This boundless love is a reminder of my divine connection and the love that my Heavenly Father has for each of us. I am thankful for the love that uplifts me in times of need, fills my heart with joy, and serves as a constant source of strength. In gratitude, I strive to reflect this love back into the world, knowing that through it, I can make a lasting and positive impact on those around me.

I live in a state of gratitude, and my life reflects this.

1 THESSALONIANS 5:18 (NIV)

"GIVE THANKS IN ALL CIRCUMSTANCES; FOR THIS IS GOD'S WILL FOR YOU IN CHRIST JESUS."

I wholeheartedly embrace a life immersed in gratitude, and the beauty of this choice radiates throughout my every moment. Gratitude has become the lens through which I view the world, allowing me to recognize blessings in even the smallest details of life.

In this state of thankfulness, I find contentment, joy, and a profound sense of peace. It shapes my interactions, infuses my relationships with warmth, and empowers me to face challenges with unwavering resilience.

My life is a testament to the revitalizing energy of gratitude, and I am endlessly grateful for the abundant blessings it bestows upon me.

Each day, I am filled with gratitude for the blessings of my life, and I pay it forward to others.

PSALM 107:1 (NIV)

"GIVE THANKS TO THE LORD, FOR HE IS GOOD; HIS LOVE ENDURES FOREVER."

Every day, my heart overflows with gratitude for the countless blessings that grace my life. This profound sense of thankfulness fuels my desire to share that abundance with others. True abundance isn't measured by what I possess but by what I give.

As I receive the gift of grace and blessings from God, I am inspired to pay it forward, extending a helping hand, a kind word, or a listening ear to those in need.

This act of giving and gratitude creates a beautiful cycle of positivity, allowing the blessings to multiply and touch the lives of those around me. In this way, I not only receive but also give, and together we experience the true richness of life.

Let your Life be affirmed

December:

Renewed Focus and Energy For The New Year

Walking in Your Authenticity and Divine Blessings as you Prepare for Another Year

This month's affirmations are centered on renewal, focusing our minds and hearts on the promise of a fresh start in the upcoming year. You have accomplished so much this year. You have been consistent with your affirmations. You have loved on yourself, you have loved on others, and you have dedicated yourself to being the best version of yourself in every way. Take a second to celebrate and be proud of yourself!

As this year ends, I encourage you to enhance your focus on your goals, your purpose, and your dreams. Renew your energy as you get ready to catapult your dreams into reality.

You are closer now than you were at the start of the year. I pray that this journey has been transformative and deeply impactful for you!

I cannot wait to see the mighty ways that God shines in your life!

YOU ARE AFFIRMED!

I am committed to my goals and take consistent action towards them.

2 CORINTHIANS 5:17 (ESV)

"THEREFORE, IF ANYONE IS IN CHRIST, HE IS A NEW CREATION. THE OLD HAS PASSED AWAY; BEHOLD, THE NEW HAS COME."

I am unalterable in my commitment to my goals, knowing that they are in alignment with God's plan for my life. I understand that achieving these goals requires consistent action and dedication. Each day, I take purposeful steps forward, fueled by my faith and determination.

I remain steadfast in my pursuit. I know that with God's guidance and my persistent effort, I can turn my dreams into reality.

My commitment is not only to myself but to the purpose and calling that God has placed within me, and I am willing to put in the work to see it come to fruition.

Renewal and transformation start within, and I embrace change wholeheartedly.

ISAIAH 43:18-19 (ESV)

"REMEMBER NOT THE FORMER THINGS, NOR CONSIDER THE THINGS OF OLD. BEHOLD, I AM DOING A NEW THING; NOW IT SPRINGS FORTH, DO I NOT PERCEIVE IT? I WILL MAKE A WAY IN THE WILDERNESS AND RIVERS IN THE DESERT."

Renewal and transformation are not external processes; they begin within the depths of my heart and soul. I wholeheartedly embrace change as a catalyst for growth and spiritual evolution.

With God's guidance, I am open to shedding old habits, beliefs, and limitations that no longer serve me. I welcome the opportunity to become a better version of myself each day.

I am a vessel for positive change, and I eagerly embrace the journey of renewal and transformation that unfolds within me.

I don't wait for a new year; I initiate change at any moment I choose.

ISAIAH 43:19 (ESV)

"BEHOLD, I AM DOING A NEW THING; NOW IT SPRINGS FORTH, DO YOU NOT PERCEIVE IT? I WILL MAKE A WAY IN THE WILDERNESS AND RIVERS IN THE DESERT."

I don't limit myself to the constraints of a new year; instead, I recognize that the power to initiate change resides within me at any given moment. Every breath I take challenges me to lean into transformation and growth.

I am not bound by the calendar, for each day brings the chance to set new intentions, pursue fresh goals, and embrace positive change. With faith as my compass, I boldly step into the unknown, knowing that the present moment is the perfect time to initiate the positive shifts I desire.

I am the author of my own narrative, and I seize every moment for transformation and renewal.

My focus and determination propel me towards success.

PSALM 37:5 (ESV)

"COMMIT YOUR WAY TO THE LORD; TRUST IN HIM, AND HE WILL ACT."

My focus is a laser that cuts through distractions, and my determination is the driving force behind my journey to success. I understand that success is not wishful thinking but deliberate action and steadfast commitment.

I set clear goals, maintain laser vision, and persevere through challenges. With faith as my foundation, I know that my focus and determination are the wings that will carry me to new heights.

Every day, I take purposeful steps toward my dreams, guided by the awareness that success is not a destination; it's a journey that I'm fully equipped to embrace.

I am the architect of my destiny, shaping it with intention and purpose.

1 CORINTHIANS 9:24 (ESV)

"DO YOU NOT KNOW THAT IN A RACE ALL THE RUNNERS RUN, BUT ONLY ONE RECEIVES THE PRIZE? SO RUN THAT YOU MAY OBTAIN IT."

I am the architect of my destiny, with the power to design a life filled with intention and purpose. Guided by my faith and determination, I lay the foundation of my dreams and construct each day with purposeful actions.

I understand that life's circumstances may present challenges, but I view them as opportunities to refine my design and make it even more resilient.

With God as my ultimate partner in this architectural journey, I am equipped with the tools to construct a life that not only serves me but also inspires and uplifts those around me.

Change begins with a single decision, and I am empowered to choose.

PROVERBS 16:3 (ESV)

"COMMIT YOUR WORK TO THE LORD, AND YOUR PLANS WILL BE ESTABLISHED."

Change is a powerful force that starts with a single decision, and I fully embrace my empowerment to choose. Each day, I recognize the opportunities before me and the potential for transformation they hold.

Through prayer, faith, and a steadfast commitment to growth, I take those decisive steps toward positive change. With God's guidance as my compass, I navigate the path of transformation with increasing faith and the understanding that my choices shape the life I desire.

I release the past and step into a brighter future with clarity.

JOSHUA 1:9 (ESV)

"HAVE I NOT COMMANDED YOU? BE STRONG AND COURAGEOUS. DO NOT BE FRIGHTENED, AND DO NOT BE DISMAYED, FOR THE LORD YOUR GOD IS WITH YOU WHEREVER YOU GO."

I wholeheartedly release the past, freeing myself from its grip, and step into a brighter future with crystal-clear clarity. Through prayer and faith, I've learned that dwelling on the past only hinders my progress and keeps me from fully embracing the blessings that await me.

I am determined to walk forward with my eyes fixed on the path ahead, guided by God's light.

My commitment to growth knows no bounds; I am limitless.

PSALM 34:4 (ESV)

"I SOUGHT THE LORD, AND HE ANSWERED ME AND DELIVERED ME FROM ALL MY FEARS."

My commitment to growth is unwavering, and I believe that with God, I am truly limitless. Through faith, I've come to understand that my potential is boundless when I align myself with divine purpose.

With God by my side, there is no challenge too great and no dream too ambitious.

I am not defined by my circumstances; I am defined by my choices.

ISAIAH 30:21(ESV)

"AND YOUR EARS SHALL HEAR A WORD BEHIND YOU, SAYING, 'THIS IS THE WAY, WALK IN IT,' WHEN YOU TURN TO THE RIGHT OR WHEN YOU TURN TO THE LEFT."

My identity is not shaped by the circumstances that surround me but rather by the choices I make in response to those circumstances. I inspire others to recognize the power of their own choices.

With God's guidance, I can rise above adversity, transform challenges into opportunities, and chart a path toward a purpose-driven life. It's through my choices that I discover my true self and unlock the potential for remarkable growth and fulfillment.

Each day is an opportunity to align with my purpose and passion.

PHILIPPIANS 3:12 (ESV)

"NOT THAT I HAVE ALREADY OBTAINED THIS OR AM ALREADY PERFECT, BUT I PRESS ON TO MAKE IT MY OWN BECAUSE CHRIST JESUS HAS MADE ME HIS OWN."

Every morning, I wake up with a sense of purpose and an unwavering passion to inspire and uplift others. Each day is a new opportunity to align myself with God's divine plan for my life and to serve as a vessel of His love and guidance. I believe that by embracing this daily opportunity, I can make a meaningful impact on those I encounter, helping them discover their own purpose and passion along the way. With faith as my compass, I walk this journey with gratitude, knowing that every day is a gift meant to be lived with intention and enthusiasm.

I welcome challenges as steppingstones to my ultimate success.

PSALM 119:10 (ESV)

"WITH MY WHOLE HEART, I SEEK YOU; LET ME NOT WANDER FROM YOUR COMMANDMENTS!"

Challenges are not obstacles; they are strategic, divinely placed stones that lead me to my ultimate success. With each challenge, I grow stronger, wiser, and more resilient. I embrace them with open arms, knowing that they are opportunities in disguise.

Through faith and determination, I navigate these challenges, confident that they are shaping me into the person I am destined to become. I welcome them as part of my journey, for they are the very stones that pave the way to my highest achievements.

I am resilient, adaptable, and fully capable of achieving my goals.

JEREMIAH 29:11 (ESV)

"FOR I KNOW THE PLANS I HAVE FOR YOU, DECLARES THE LORD, PLANS FOR WELFARE AND NOT FOR EVIL, TO GIVE YOU A FUTURE AND A HOPE."

I am resilient, adaptable, and fully capable of achieving my goals. Life's twists and turns only strengthen my resolve and reveal my true potential. I embrace change as an opportunity to learn, grow, and evolve.

With faith and a determined spirit, I navigate every challenge, knowing that I have the inner strength to overcome.

My goals are not just aspirations; they are destinations waiting to be reached. I trust in my abilities and keep moving forward, for I am resilient, adaptable, and fully capable of manifesting my dreams into reality.

The power to transform my life rests within me, and I harness it now.

PSALM 51:6 (ESV)

"BEHOLD, YOU DELIGHT IN TRUTH IN THE INWARD BEING, AND YOU TEACH ME WISDOM IN THE SECRET HEART."

The power to transform my life rests within me, and I harness it now. I understand that the key to unlocking my full potential lies in my thoughts, actions, and choices.

With faith as my guide and determination as my fuel, I take charge of my destiny. Each day is an opportunity to shape the life I desire.

I embrace this power within, knowing that I have the capacity to create the positive change I seek. My journey is marked by purpose, intention, and the victory that comes with knowing that I am the master of my destiny.

I am not limited by time; I create change in the present moment.

PSALM 19:14 (ESV)

"LET THE WORDS OF MY MOUTH AND THE MEDITATION OF MY HEART BE ACCEPTABLE IN YOUR SIGHT, O LORD, MY ROCK, AND MY REDEEMER."

I am not limited by time; I create change in the present moment. I understand that waiting for the perfect time or a specific date is not necessary for transformation. Every second, every breath, is an opportunity for growth and renewal. I seize the power of the now to make choices that align with my goals and purpose.

Time is my ally, and I use it wisely to shape my destiny and live a life of intention and significance. Today, I take action, for the present is where change begins, and I am its author.

Renewed focus and commitment are my daily companions.

ROMANS 8:31 (ESV)

"WHAT THEN SHALL WE SAY TO THESE THINGS? IF GOD IS FOR US, WHO CAN BE AGAINST US?"

Renewed focus and commitment are my daily companions. I understand that achieving my goals and living a purpose-driven life requires consistent dedication. Each morning, I awaken with a fresh sense of purpose, ready to tackle the day with fierce determination.

I embrace the power of intention, and I choose to channel my energy toward my dreams and aspirations. With every step I take, I affirm my commitment to growth and success, with the inner strength to overcome any obstacle that may come my way.

Each day is an opportunity to reaffirm my dedication to living my best life.

I am the author of my life story, and I write it with intention.

ROMANS 12:2 (ESV)

"DO NOT BE CONFORMED TO THIS WORLD, BUT BE TRANSFORMED BY THE RENEWAL OF YOUR MIND, THAT BY TESTING YOU MAY DISCERN WHAT IS THE WILL OF GOD, WHAT IS GOOD AND ACCEPTABLE AND PERFECT."

I am the author of my life story, and I write it with intention and purpose. Each day, I hold the pen, ready to craft the chapters of my journey. I understand that while life may present unexpected twists and turns, I have the power to shape my narrative.

With faith as my guiding star, I write a story filled with hope, resilience, and love. Every word I choose reflects my values, dreams, and the legacy I wish to leave behind.

I am intentional in my choices, and I trust that with each stroke of the pen, my life story becomes a testament to faith, growth, and choosing the power of a purpose-driven life.

I celebrate every step of my journey, no matter how small.

PSALM 51:10 (ESV)

"CREATE IN ME A CLEAN HEART, O GOD, AND RENEW A RIGHT SPIRIT WITHIN ME."

I celebrate every step of my journey, no matter how small. Each moment, each achievement, and each obstacle overcome is a reason for gratitude and joy. Life is a collection of these small victories, and I choose to acknowledge and cherish them all.

It's in these seemingly ordinary moments that I find the beauty of life's wonders stitched with threads of faith, perseverance, and love.

By celebrating every step, I create a life filled with a sense of fulfillment and purpose, and I recognize that every moment is a gift from God to be cherished and embraced.

My goals are not dreams; they are my reality in the making.

PSALM 51:12 (ESV)

"RESTORE TO ME THE JOY OF YOUR SALVATION, AND UPHOLD ME WITH A WILLING SPIRIT."

My goals are not dreams; they are my reality in the making. I believe in the power of faith, hard work, and perseverance to turn my aspirations into tangible achievements. Every day, I take steps toward my goals with tenacious determination, knowing that they are not distant fantasies but concrete destinations on my journey.

Through prayer, dedication, and focused action, I bring my goals to life, aligning my path with God's divine plan. With this mindset, I manifest my dreams into reality, and I trust that God's guidance will lead me to the fulfillment of every goal I set my heart on.

I am a force of change, and I embrace it with open arms.

COLOSSIANS 3:10 (ESV)

"AND HAVE PUT ON THE NEW SELF, WHICH IS BEING RENEWED IN KNOWLEDGE AFTER THE IMAGE OF ITS CREATOR."

I am a force of change, and I embrace it with open arms. Change is the vehicle of growth and transformation, and I understand its vital role in my journey. Instead of fearing change, I welcome it as an opportunity to evolve, learn, and become the best version of myself.

With faith as my compass and determination as my driving force, I navigate the seas of change with courage and grace. I trust that every twist and turn on life's path leads me to a brighter future. I am ready to embrace the changes that lead me to my purpose and destiny.

I am inspired by the possibilities that each new moment brings.

PSALM 119:105 (ESV)

"YOUR WORD IS A LAMP TO MY FEET AND A LIGHT TO MY PATH."

The possibilities that each new moment brings inspire me. Life is a journey filled with infinite opportunities waiting to be discovered. With every breath I take, I am reminded of the boundless potential that lies within me and around me.

I approach each day with an open heart and a hopeful spirit, knowing that each new moment is a chance to create, learn, and grow. The beauty of life is that it constantly offers us a fresh canvas to paint our dreams and aspirations.

I am deeply grateful for the inspiration that surrounds me, and I eagerly embrace the endless possibilities that each new day presents.

I trust in my ability to overcome obstacles and achieve greatness.

1 TIMOTHY 6:17 (NASB1995)

"INSTRUCT THOSE WHO ARE RICH IN THIS PRESENT WORLD NOT TO BE CONCEITED OR TO FIX THEIR HOPE ON THE UNCERTAINTY OF RICHES, BUT ON GOD, WHO RICHLY SUPPLIES US WITH ALL THINGS TO ENJOY."

I trust in my ability to overcome obstacles and achieve greatness. Life may present challenges and hurdles, but I believe that within me lies the strength and resilience to conquer them.

With unwavering faith and determination, I navigate the twists and turns of my journey, knowing that each obstacle is an opportunity in disguise. I embrace these challenges, and I am confident that my spirit is indomitable.

My trust in God's guidance and my own capabilities propels me forward, allowing me to rise above adversity and reach the heights of greatness that await me.

I am unwavering in my commitment to my vision and purpose.

PHILIPPIANS 3:13-14 (ESV)

"BROTHERS, I DO NOT CONSIDER THAT I HAVE MADE IT MY OWN. BUT ONE THING I DO: FORGETTING WHAT LIES BEHIND AND STRAINING FORWARD TO WHAT LIES AHEAD, I PRESS ON TOWARD THE GOAL FOR THE PRIZE OF THE UPWARD CALL OF GOD IN CHRIST JESUS."

Every day, I wake up with a clear sense of direction and an unshakeable determination to pursue my calling. I understand that my purpose is a divine gift, and I am entrusted with the responsibility to fulfill it.

Regardless of the challenges and distractions that may come my way, I stay focused on my mission, guided by my faith and the knowledge that I am walking the path that God has set before me.

My commitment is resolute, and I know that with perseverance, faith, and dedication, I will see my vision manifest.

I am the master of my destiny, shaping it with each choice I make.

GENESIS 1:26 (NASB1995)

"THEN GOD SAID, "LET US MAKE MAN IN OUR IMAGE, ACCORDING TO OUR LIKENESS; AND LET THEM RULE OVER THE FISH OF THE SEA AND OVER THE BIRDS OF THE SKY AND OVER THE CATTLE AND OVER ALL THE EARTH, AND OVER EVERY CREEPING THING THAT CREEPS ON THE EARTH."

Every decision I make, whether big or small, contributes to the course of my life's journey. I recognize the power that lies within me to steer my life in the direction I desire.

With each choice, I am deliberate and mindful, knowing that my actions have consequences. I choose faith over fear, love over hate, and growth over stagnation.

In the hands of God, I craft a life filled with purpose, abundance, and fulfillment, understanding that I have the ability to manifest my dreams through the choices I make along the way.

I am not bound by the past; I am propelled by the future.

HEBREWS 6:19 (ESV)

"WE HAVE THIS AS A SURE AND STEADFAST ANCHOR OF THE SOUL, A HOPE THAT ENTERS INTO THE INNER PLACE BEHIND THE CURTAIN."

I am not bound by the past; I am propelled by the future. The mistakes and experiences of yesterday do not define who I am today or dictate where I'm heading. Instead, I use them as steppingstones toward a brighter and more purposeful future.

I carry the lessons learned from my past as wisdom, not as burdens. With steadfast faith in God's guidance, I eagerly embrace the endless possibilities that lie ahead.

Each new day I move forward, grow, and manifest the destiny I envision. In the hands of the Divine, my future is filled with hope, promise, and boundless potential.

I rejoice for the birth of the Savior.

MATTHEW 1:21-23 (NIV)

"SHE WILL GIVE BIRTH TO A SON, AND YOU ARE TO GIVE HIM THE NAME JESUS, BECAUSE HE WILL SAVE HIS PEOPLE FROM THEIR SINS. ALL THIS TOOK PLACE TO FULFILL WHAT THE LORD HAD SAID THROUGH THE PROPHET:

The virgin will conceive and give birth to a son, and they will call him Immanuel, which means "God with us."

In the heart of this sacred season, I give praise for the profound gift of Jesus Christ, whose arrival brought hope, love, and redemption to the world.

His birth is the manifested promise of God's boundless love for us, and it fills my heart with gratitude and joy. As I celebrate the birth of our Savior, I embrace His teachings of love, compassion, and forgiveness in my own life.

This season is a reminder of the incredible blessings that come from God's grace, and I am truly thankful for the presence of Jesus in my journey of faith.

I choose to become a better version of myself each day.

ISAIAH 41:10 (ESV)

"FEAR NOT, FOR I AM WITH YOU; BE NOT DISMAYED, FOR I AM YOUR GOD; I WILL STRENGTHEN YOU, I WILL HELP YOU, I WILL UPHOLD YOU WITH MY RIGHTEOUS RIGHT HAND."

I choose to become a better version of myself each day. This journey of growth and self-improvement is not bound by time or limitations. With each sunrise, I am granted a fresh opportunity to align my actions, thoughts, and intentions with the person I aspire to be.

I rely on God's grace and guidance to help me shed old habits and embrace new ones, to let go of what no longer serves me, and to welcome positive changes. Every decision I make, every lesson I learn, and every step I take is a testament to my commitment to constant improvement.

As I evolve, I become a living example of God's transformative power, inspiring others to embark on their own journeys of self-discovery and elevation.

I am motivated by the potential for positive change in every moment.

LAMENTATIONS 3:22-23 (ESV)

"THE STEADFAST LOVE OF THE LORD NEVER CEASES; HIS MERCIES NEVER COME TO AN END; THEY ARE NEW EVERY MORNING; GREAT IS YOUR FAITHFULNESS."

I am motivated by the potential for positive change in every moment of my life. Each day is filled with opportunities to grow, learn, and make a difference.

With faith as my foundation and determination as my driving force, I embrace the power of choice to create the change I desire. I understand that every decision I make can lead to a brighter and more purposeful future.

Through prayer, reflection, and a heart full of gratitude, I harness this motivation to seize each moment and contribute to the greater good.

I am an instrument of positive change, driven by the belief that transformation is possible at any time, and I am committed to making the most of every moment.

I am the catalyst for transformation in my life, and I embrace it.

EPHESIANS 4:22-24 (ESV)

"PUT OFF YOUR OLD SELF, WHICH BELONGS TO YOUR FORMER MANNER OF LIFE AND IS CORRUPT THROUGH DECEITFUL DESIRES, AND TO BE RENEWED IN THE SPIRIT OF YOUR MINDS, AND TO PUT ON THE NEW SELF, CREATED AFTER THE LIKENESS OF GOD IN TRUE RIGHTEOUSNESS AND HOLINESS."

I am the catalyst for transformation in my life, and I embrace it with open arms. I understand that change is an essential part of growth, and I welcome it as an opportunity to become the best version of myself.

With God as my guide and my boundless faith, I am empowered to initiate and navigate this transformative journey. I trust in His divine plan for a brighter, more purposeful future.

Through prayer, self-reflection, and a heart full of gratitude, I continue to evolve and grow, embracing transformation as a beautiful and necessary process on my path to success and fulfillment.

Success is my birthright, and I claim it with unwavering commitment.

ISAIAH 40:31 (ESV)

"BUT THEY WHO WAIT FOR THE LORD SHALL RENEW THEIR STRENGTH; THEY SHALL MOUNT UP WITH WINGS LIKE EAGLES; THEY SHALL RUN AND NOT BE WEARY; THEY SHALL WALK AND NOT FAINT."

Success is my birthright, and I claim it with steady commitment. I understand that God has equipped me with the potential for greatness, and I am called to fulfill that purpose.

With faith, determination, and a heart full of gratitude, I walk the path toward success. I embrace challenges as opportunities to learn and grow, knowing that setbacks are simply setups for future victories.

I am resilient, adaptable, and fully capable of achieving my goals. Success is not a destination; it's a journey, and I am on that journey with unwavering faith in God's plan for my life.

I don't wait for a new year; I seize every moment as an opportunity for renewal and growth.

2 CORINTHIANS 4:16 (ESV)

"SO WE DO NOT LOSE HEART. THOUGH OUR OUTER SELF IS WASTING AWAY, OUR INNER SELF IS BEING RENEWED DAY BY DAY."

Time is a gift, and I understand that waiting for a specific date to initiate change is unnecessary. Each day brings a chance to renew my commitment to personal development, to embrace positive change, and to grow in faith and purpose.

I am the architect of my destiny, shaping it with intention and determination, regardless of the calendar. Each moment is a fresh start, a blank canvas, and I am ready to paint a masterpiece of growth, love, and transformation.

I am empowered. I am enough. I am affirmed.

PROVERBS 4:25 (ESV)

"LET YOUR EYES LOOK DIRECTLY FORWARD, AND YOUR GAZE BE STRAIGHT BEFORE YOU."

I am so proud of myself for committing to my daily affirmations. I can see the positive changes that have taken place throughout the past 12 months. My confidence in God and myself have increased exponentially. I feel more motivated than ever before to achieve my dreams, to use my God-given gifts and abilities to impact the world and to become the best version of myself.

These words resonate within my being as a constant reminder of my inherent worth and potential. I understand that true empowerment comes from embracing my authenticity and recognizing that I am fully equipped to navigate life's challenges.

I release the need for external validation and embrace the truth that I am enough just as I am. Each day, I affirm my worth and step into the world with confidence, knowing that I am affirmed by a higher purpose and divine love. This affirmation fuels my journey and propels me towards my goals with unwavering faith.

You Are
Affirmed!

About the Author

Dr. Cheryl Polote-Williamson is a nationally acclaimed multi-best-selling *author*, **Editor-in-Chief of Cheryl Magazine,** award-winning filmmaker and executive producer, transformational speaker, and certified success coach.

Williamson is the CEO and Founder of Williamson Media Group, LLC, and Cheryl Polote-Williamson, LLC, where her knowledge, expertise, and resources connect others to their purpose. As a global leader, she has successfully ushered 470 men and women into thriving entrepreneurship.

In December 2021, Dr. Williamson received her Honorary Doctor of Philosophy. She has also received multiple national and international media features and mentions and several awards for her leadership capabilities, including selection as one of Dallas Top 25 women and the honor as one of the **Female Success Factor Award** recipients for 2**016, the 2017 and 2018 Indie Author Literary Trailblazer Award, Global Smashers**

Award, Who's Who in Black Dallas Publishing, and **Indie Author Legacy Award in 2017** and **2018,** a **2018 African American Literary Award,** a **2020 African American Literary Award for Self-Published Author of the Year Award,** and a **2021 Trailblazer Award in Media**.

Williamson is a highly sought-after influencer and business leader who is also the Founder and CEO of **Soul Reborn,** a 501(c)(3) non-profit charitable organization that has supported more than 10,000 disenfranchised, under-served, and previously incarcerated women through lectures, classes, summits, and conferences on leadership, entrepreneurship, money management, etiquette, storytelling, and philanthropy.

Serving is Cheryl Polote-Williamson's passion, but nothing comes before the love and care she gives to her husband Russ Williamson of 30 years, her three amazing children, Russ, Jr., Courtney, and Lauren, and two adorable grandbabies, Leah and Russ III.

To learn more, visit her website at www.cherylpwilliamson.com

Printed in the USA
CPSIA information can be obtained
at www.ICGtesting.com
LVHW011147081024
793246LV00011B/383